CW01017660

AMICABLE SPIRITUALISM

By

Sidney Pickersgill

CON-PSY PUBLICATIONS

First Edition

© Sidney Pickersgill
2015

Published by
CON-PSY PUBLICATIONS

P.O. BOX 14,
GREENFORD,
MIDDLESEX, UB6 0UF.

ISBN 978 1 898680 72 7

DEDICATION

To my wife, Joyce. Without her encouragement this book may never have been written and acknowledging the saying 'behind every good man is a good woman'.

When I sit at my laptop not wanting to write, whether I like it or not, they will do so. My Inspires cast their inspirations upon me and I submit to them as far as my ability allows. After that it's up to them to take over. I do not become unconscious but it's as if I am a musical instrument in the hands of some superior power and attuned to their touch. Then, I have to put the thoughts into action in case I lose contact.

ABOUT THE AUTHOR

Sidney Pickersgill was born in 1931 in a small mining village near Wakefield in Yorkshire. His father, a miner, was a staunch Methodist, his mother a Salvationist and Sid sang in the local church choir.

He attended local schools until at the age of fourteen and then began work as a 'clicker' in the local boot and clog factory. Following four years of National Service in the army, where he was kept at 'Base' because of his skills in repairing equipment, he returned to the factory but soon joined his friends down the local pit, where the pay was better.

Four years later, seeking a better life for his growing family, they emigrated to Australia but returned, for family reasons, after only three years. He later met and married Joyce and they brought up his family of three boys together.

He has been a member of Wakefield Spiritualist Church for over fifty years, serving as secretary and then, for seventeen years, as President. He now holds the title of Honorary President and has the Long Service Award of the Spiritualists' National Union.

His first love has always been healing, becoming a member of Castleford Healing Group in 1960. He attended their Easter Rally, where he met the secretary of Wakefield Church, Mr Horace Wright, who took him back to Wakefield and made him a member there. Joyce and Sid both hold the healing diploma of the SNU, working in church and with the public and also attending hospitals and for fourteen years was a Chaplin at HMP Wakefield and Full Sutton. For forty years as a certificated speaker and demonstrator, Sid has served churches all around the country with his wife Joyce.

CONTENTS

ABOUT OURSELVES

SELF-DOUBT

Every time the postman delivers a letter, even before it is opened, we begin to wonder what it contains; what new problem, what news, good or bad. It seems that the Great Arranger of all things felt that problems were essential to human growth and development, otherwise He would never allow so many things to worry us.

I am also convinced that the Great Creator planted in each of us capabilities to deal with our problems. What then prevents so many people from reaching their own solutions?

It's not lack of education or intelligence, it must be that they have certain roadblocks in their mind, or some physical obstacle, that limit their abilities. There are many things that cast a shadow over problem-ridden people... and one is Self-Doubt.

The best way to solve your problems is to believe in yourself, believe that you yourself can solve them, A great man, Emerson, said: "A man is what he thinks about all day long." If he thinks success, he creates it, but if he thinks failure, he will set the stage for it. Self-doubt makes people afraid to stand up to their problems, but the truth is that when you stand up to your difficulties, very often your difficulties will not stand up to you.

The author of this poem, Ron DeMarco, writes:

I'VE DREAMED MANY DREAMS

I've dreamed many dreams that never came true.
I've seen them vanish at dawn.
But I've realized enough of my dreams thank the Lord,
To make me want to dream on.
I've prayed many prayers, when no answers came,
Though I've waited patient and long,
But answers have come to enough of my prayers
To make me keep praying on.

9

I've trusted many a friend that failed,
And left me to weep alone,
But I've found enough of my friends that are really true,
That will make me keep trusting on.

I've sown many seeds that have fallen by the way,
For the birds to feed upon,
But I've held enough golden sheaves in my hands,
To make me keep sowing on.

I've drunk from the cup of disappointment and pain
I've gone many days without song,
But I've sipped enough nectar from the Roses of life
To make me keep living on!

So if you meet a self-doubting person, say to them: "You have come a long way in this difficult world, with all its difficult situations and you are still functioning" and remind them that the best way to forget their problems is to help someone else with theirs. They may find that they have more courage and strength than they think they had. I say to self-doubting people: "Meditate on the poem."

RESENTMENT is the next part of our problems. It is a state of mind that destroys love and creates suffering and can very often result in the failings of someone else who may have said a spiteful word or done a hateful thing and left us bitter, hurt and angry. Carrying a load of anger around with you wastes your energy and blocks communications. If you have a feeling of intense bitterness towards someone, first you must be reconciled with them, but the only permanent answer is forgiveness. This may take time. My parents taught us that it was useless to pray with resentment in our hearts.

GUILT is the next part of our problems. Religion teaches us that the only way to deal with a guilt problem is to regret the offence, resolve not to repeat it, make amends if possible and ask forgiveness from the person you have wronged and forget it. If you do these things the wound in your mind will heal cleanly and leave no scar, but many people will not follow this blueprint and will go on being poisoned by guilty feelings. Forgiveness is a gradual process, so if you do not attempt forgiveness the only person you are hurting is yourself.

Feeling guilty can be depressing and keep you from moving forward with your life. It is one of the worst emotions a human can carry. How does one get rid of guilt? Talking to someone may help. Time, the great healer, usually makes your guilt fade away.

You have to realise that you cannot change anything you did a minute ago, let alone years ago. You apologise to whoever, including yourself and work on not making the same mistakes. Remember everyone is human, I would not find this task easy myself.

Each of us is a life, a mind and Spirit. The inner change means that everything touching your life may be assimilated into spiritual power.

WORRY is the most common problem on this, our material Earth. A wise man said: "It is like a thin stream of fear trickling through the mind" and if it is encouraged it will cut a channel into which all other thoughts are drained. Dozens of people worry about their health. One person I know was convinced that she would die of cancer because her mother and grandmother had died from it (hence a worry). But, you know, the truth is that most fears and disasters will never take place. In any case, worrying will do nothing to prevent it.

One remedy for excessive worry is a clear understanding of how much emotional and physical damage it can do to you. It can affect your heart and your glands; in fact, the whole nervous system. Never has anyone died of hard work, but many with worry.

Most people try to help themselves by keeping themselves occupied; they dig the garden, read, knit or just go for a walk, anything except sit at home and brood If you can change the setting you can usually change the mood. The song says, "I live one day at a time." That is the best antidote for worry. Problems? The world will continue to be full of them, but we should not complain or despair. Challenge and response, that is what life is, That is where its greatest triumphs and fulfilments lie. So sweep away self-doubt, resentment, guilt and worry and you will be amazed how the strength and joy come flooding in.

So why worry? Worry gets you nowhere at all.

TRUTH

First, we have to look at ourselves and say: "Am I truthful?" I am afraid many people say that they never tell untruths, but truth does not end at that, truth is a word with more than one meaning. God said: I have no greater joy than to hear that my children walk in truth," for that is what religion is all about. First, be truthful to each other; it's no good attending your place of worship unless you can say: "I love you all who attend with me" and mean it truthfully, so try to the best of your abilities to help other people along life's way. I say this because I know that I could never have taken the platform unless others had given me a hand.

Since through this great truth enlightening, I have proved all life divine. God is ever present, filling now this life of mine.

SINFULNESS

I think that the Fifth Principle of Spiritualism teaches us that we are personally responsible for all that we do in this life, good or bad and that we cannot place our wrongdoings onto someone else's shoulders. We have to work at our advancement in the next life, but we could start our progression at any time - the sooner the better,

I think we all have failed the test, for I'm sure that we all have done something in our lifetime that we regret; Islam teaches that it is an avoidable act that harms the perpetrator's own soul.

My father, a good Methodist, would tell the family that God created everything for us to enjoy but he did not say we could abuse it because when we do it becomes sinful. Spiritual progression is wholly dependent upon the individual and it is very important that we keep control of our thoughts and actions.

As we are given freedom of choice (free will), so also are we given the ability to recognise what is right from what is wrong.

FAITH

Many times have I heard it said that "faith can move mountains." You might say it would need a terrific amount of faith to do this but that is what faith is - believing in the impossible. Many times you have heard it said: "If at first you don't succeed, try again", but it's no good trying at all if you have no faith.

"Cherish faith in one another, When you meet in friendships name" is a hymn we sing. I would say that this kind of faith is the most priceless thing on Earth, but to have faith in God, who you have never seen, then this, my friends, is indeed the most precious gem with a price no man could pay if a charge was made. Faith isn't believing without proof, it's trusting without reservation.

Mother Teresa said: "Be faithful in small things because it is in them that your strength lies." You will only succeed in whatever you want to do if you convince yourself you can succeed in it.

How soon things become a memory, how swiftly time steals away the moments, the days, the weeks, the years. What is the lesson it teaches? What things can be remembered by the everlasting waves of thought? The joys of the present go quickly and slip away into the past. As I grow older, I want to linger longer in peaceful situations, to stand on the edge of a cliff and watch the sunlight dance over the valley below, or to watch the sparkling silver waves, hear the rustling leaves that dance in the breeze. All bring music to my ears. As the day grows to a close, today will be yesterday, so now is the time of life when my mind records more often the magical, enchanting beauty of the heart's moving moments. What a world of memories.

AS I SEE IT

It is easier for speakers of other religions to prepare or speak on their religion. For all through the year the Christian religions have some occasion to celebrate. Of course, we all observe Christmas, but the Christian calendar is followed by, Good Friday, Easter Day, Whit Sunday, Advent, Lent, Ascension, Holy Trinity and more.

So, it's not difficult for Christian speakers to prepare a service; also, the congregation know the celebration and they expect the Minister, Parson, etc. to preach to them a service on that particular event, at that time of the year, so the theme is chosen for them. In between, they have all the Gospel stories, the parables and Commandments. All these give their congregation a rich, varied and sustaining diet of Christian truths. These are prepared and delivered on all the great festivals; they realise that to preach something different would be robbing the congregation of their Christian beliefs, yet every year the same stories are told and faithfully accepted by the Christian people,

My question here would be: Do they ever ask themselves why they need to hear them? These stories have been told over and over again and therefore perhaps distort the truth. Now we must ask what kind of a service do we as Spiritualists want to hear from the rostrum. Recently, a friend of mine said he had attended our churches all around the country and not once had he heard a service where God was spoken of. He had heard more than once a service on thoughts are living things. Now, I realise that if we are going to speak about God, or interpret the word of God, then we must understand more about God ourselves. The Christian Ministers have a much easier task, for they can tell their congregation that God speaks to them through the pages of the Bible, but many Church of England Ministers now question is there a God.

I see Spiritualism and its philosophy as the baker whose task it is to make available to the public the best bread that he can possibly produce, and in doing so he will use all and every advantage that is known to him in order that the bread will be pure and wholesome and free from all impurities.

It is now the shop assistant's job to sell the loaf; she will not tell you how it is made but will express that you are buying the best bread, with no impurities, for the price you pay. (If you want the best, you have to pay for it.)

In some ways we are the salesperson and the bread our religion. We want the best product to sell to the public, so what can we do to make our services better? We have to make it clear that SNU Spiritualism can be good and wholesome. That is up to each and every one of us, for no one can even begin to feel good unless a change is brought about within ourselves. You cannot fool the Spirit World with pretence for there is a constant stress on the fact that morality is an integral part of religion. The church can offer you the facilities, but you must do the work of your own restoration.

All religions are fishing for people to join them; they all hope that they are using the right bait. The catch may be large or small and they may catch some fish that they do not want and have to throw them back into the sea of life. Sometimes the look of the catch will not seem much for all the hard work put in to landing it, and sometimes the big one will almost pull you out of the boat and you realise it's best to cut it loose and let it go.

Here, we must draw the distinction between what people need and what they want. All true teachings seem to be out of tune with today's modern lifestyle and our teachings may strike a tune of discord to them, and to speak on men's conditions does not necessary mean we say exactly what they want to hear. I realise that when I have the privilege to take a church service, and people have come to hear me speak, that they could hear and see a service without even leaving the comfort of their own homes, but the Spiritualist service is not something that can be fully understood from watching television. It has a personal encounter and response; we could never be spectators, we are participants in our church services and religion, our rostrums present the best broadcasting system and we don't make the best use of it.

Our immediate task is to drive home the message of survival after death, to comfort the mourner and help those who are ill and despairing. If we want to remain a credible movement there may have to be changes made; we cannot rely on past glories, we have to present ourselves intelligently, professionally and attractively. I'm not suggesting that we should package Spiritualism, but we should make our churches more useful in every way, a place where people want to be.

We now realise that all religions can be traced back to psychic experiences, which made our ancestors realise that other forces, other beings, though largely unseen yet, were with us when these realisations caused the understanding that there was a 'hereafter', that some power in the universe controlled Man's personal and universal destiny. "Thou great first cause least understood."

But contemplation of God's power is seen in the ever (for us) expanding immensity of the universe, all governed and in order, all inter-relating - Outer-Inner-Higher-Lower. We now know that the past stretches into infinity, so logic alone aids our convictions that our future is, likewise, without ending.

Here, our message to the world must be clear - we individuals choose, by the exercise of our free will, how much we are going to receive from participating in the adventure of life, both on this physical plane and the spiritual eternal future.

Thomas Paine described the creation as speaking a universal language, an ever-existing original which can be read and which cannot be forged or counterfeited, lost or suppressed, not by depending on the will of man, preaching to all men of all nations.

How can we further the understanding of all these truths, all fundamental to the spread of Spiritualism?

First, a careful self-analysis, whatever our age; a private and personal reaffirmation of a determination to apply a spirituality test to our daily undertakings. A resolve to lose no opportunity to broaden our experience - Educationally, Psychically, Spiritually. To realise, ourselves and then to pass on our added knowledge and experiences.

16

To travel the country, giving evidence of survival, can be your chosen vocation and you may enjoy the moment, but, in my submission, if that is all, it misses really reaching those who need us most, need our philosophy as much, if not more, than the evidence of survival. It misses the mixed up kids, the drug experimenters, the middle-aged disappointed with life legions, the elderly, the lonely, and confused, those who have just given up, or feel one of life's misfits.

TELL me not my life is sadness,
Now I've found this Truth so bright;
Every thought is filled with gladness;
Life is now one scene of light!
Calmly are the moments flying,
Free from every care and fear;
Life is one continued sunlight,
All mankind to me are dear.

Since through this great truth's enlightening,
I have proved all life divine,
God is all and ever present,
Filling now this life of mine.
Truth, eternal and immortal,
Now is dawning on our land,
Bringing peace, with joy and comfort,
Where grief reigned on every hand.

Spread the joyful tidings over
All, through earth's remotest bound;
Tell the suffering and the sorrowing,
That the way of life is found.
Truth has freed the soul, long fettered
By the power of error's chain,
And our angel friends and loved ones.
Show that Truth will ever reign.

Hymn 163 in the SNU Hymn Book.

BELIEF AND BELIEVE

Today, I just happened to hear 'The King', Elvis Presley, singing one of his hits, which I myself have always liked to hear and sing. There is a clue in the title - 'I believe'. The song inspired me to put my pen to paper and write about 'Belief and Believe', which I want to use as a guide to our religion.

First, let me tell you a story that I read in a magazine. It's about a mother who's son, Gabriel, was paralysed from the waist down. She had taken her son to see a top surgeon who, after examining him, said that he was unable to help him.

So his mum decided to take him to Lourdes and no one could believe what happened. Suddenly, to the amazement of everyone, Gabriel raised himself up to his feet and within twenty-four hours he was walking well. When he came home he was examined by several doctors and was told that he was completely cured. His mother never accepted that nothing could be done and her strong belief that her son would be healed somehow worked. (The magic of 'Belief' grants phenomenal results.)

Just think, if Isaac Watts had given up when people laughed when he told them he could use the steam kettle to move things - but he went on to give the world the steam locomotives. And even Marconi's father laughed when he told him his thoughts about electricity, but he, like Watts, believed in himself.

A person who shows some determination is a person who has a strong belief in themselves and can bring out the magic of the mind; you have the power within to make your world (your environment) just what you want it to be. Mentally, you can create a new life for yourself, whatever you believe. You can dissolve or overcome any obstacle if you believe, for belief can make you do seemingly impossible things in your life.

Another story is of a busy housewife who woke up one Monday morning, feeling like nothing on Earth, and the thought of all the housework that awaited her filled her with dread. Monday was the day she had to deal with a large family wash, followed by the ironing. Suddenly she remembered an energy tablet that her friend had given her and was assured that they were wonderful - "The best cure for tiredness". She searched through her coat pockets and found it, popped it into her mouth and started her work. The washing was child's play, she finished the ironing, cleared up, polished the floor and cleaned the windows. Life was wonderful, all from one small tablet.

She then decided to go for a walk to the local shop, put on her coat and as she walked down the garden path, put her hand in her coat pocket and guess what? YES, she found the tablet her friend had given her! What she had taken was a sweet her little girl had given her. You see, her belief brought the magic that changed her day. I think you know the answer to this short story: You are what you believe, or think you are. If things at this moment are not so good, you have to think better days are on the way and then better days will come, if you believe in yourself.

A friend of mine who lost his sight acquired an organ. He had never played any instrument before and yet he began and before long played well enough. I still have the tape he made for me before he passed into Spirit; he left a message behind. If you want to achieve something, believe it.

These are all nice stories, but what do I, as a Spiritualist, believe? First, I believe that there is no death, that life continues somewhere. Call it what you want - Heaven, paradise, the Summerland. I must bring into my belief The Seven Principles, especially the fifth one - 'Personal Responsibility'. This, I believe, tells us that we are responsible for everything we do and think in this life, that we must, in this life, do our best to prepare for the life to come. We must show that we are responsible for not only our lives but for the needs and care of all people in this world, hence the second principle, 'The Brotherhood of Man' and while we may be separated by seas and oceans, all are brothers and sisters and we are responsible for their welfare.

I realise that I have used the words 'Belief' and 'Believe' quite a few times so I looked up their meaning in the dictionary, which stated "Belief" as an "assent of the mind, persuasion, creed, opinion". Now, in Spiritualism there are no creeds and I have not found any persuasion. People who become Spiritualists do so because of need, not being persuaded by anyone to join and our opinions are not judgemental, so as to allow all to have freedom of thought.

Now "Believe" says: "To give belief to, to credit, to expect with confidence, to have a firm persuasion". Lets take "To give belief to". If the inventor Isaac Watts had to "Believe" in what he could achieve when he watched the steam kettle then that is how our thoughts should react towards our religion, so carry in your thoughts at all times the belief in your religion and what we can achieve. "Expect with confidence" that we will prove that what we teach is the TRUTH, the whole truth and nothing but the truth, with no false statements.

Which leaves us with the word "credit" and I am sure we have all at sometime in our lives have had something on credit. Now let me tell you this: The life that you are now living is on credit and one day you will have to repay the loan; YOU will have to pay for your misdoings; you cannot expect to place your responsibilities on someone else's shoulders.

It is up to each and all to progress and this progression can start at any stage in life - here whilst we are on Earth, or we can wait until we pass on, it makes no difference. If we can start our progression before we pass into Spirit it would be an asset. To help and serve others and ask no reward attracts around us conditions which are good. Remember, to give and not receive makes a life that is satisfying.

Those who leave this world and have no knowledge and have made no progress and may have rejected this fact will have to come to terms with themselves because, until they do, their progression will be slow in all senses of the word.

I suppose most of us take the belief in God for granted, others encounter a cloud in their believing.

I BELIEVE

I believe for every drop of rain that falls,
A flower grows,
I believe that somewhere in the darkest night,
A candle glows,
I believe for everyone who goes astray, someone will come,
To show the way.
I believe, I believe,

I believe above a storm, the smallest prayer,
Can still be heard,
I believe that someone in the great somewhere,
Hears every word,

Every time I here a new born baby cry,
Or touch a leaf, or see the sky,
Then I know why I believe.

Every time I here a new born baby cry,
Or touch a leaf, or see the sky,
Then I know why I believe.

Sung by Elvis Presley
(Words & music by Erwin Drake, Irvin Graham, Jimmy Shirl &
Al Stillman 1953)

CARPE DIEM

Whilst reading a book, I came across the Latin term "carpe diem", so I looked up the meaning. It translates as "seize the day" - an urgent call to live life to the fullest, getting the most out of each and every day.

I suppose it's good advice, especially for those of us who tend to live negatively and watch life pass us by. As an octogenarian, that is all that may happen, as the body goes weak, but the spirit within grows stronger and the thought-power seems to take over.

Sometimes life holds moments and even needs, and it is said that we all have five basic needs - Food, Shelter, Love, Oxygen and Clothing. Others say Food, Clothing, Shelter, Transportation and Security. "Silence" could be for one, "Speaking" for another. It depends on the person, as we all have different needs.

It is easy for the man who has all the comforts of life and has collated valuable Earthly goods. A big house, brand clothing, a new car, fancy food and drink are not needs but wants. This does not mean that you should not buy the things that you need - not at all. Life is meant to be lived, not survived, so treat yourselves to some wants along life's way, but do so when you can afford them and enjoy those wants as the little 'extras' in your life.

Enjoy the present, do not worry about tomorrow, make the best of each moment that is afforded to you; all pleasures should be enjoyed while there is still time. In other words, "make hay while the sun shines", with the empathis on making the most of your time because life is short. We become so engrossed in what we feel and hear that we operate within our natural sense rather than our spiritual ones. God's impelling spirit enables you to resist the worlds pressures, so if you do not enjoy the simple little things in life that God has given you freely, you can't enjoy spiritual realities.

So start to appreciate yourself and also the people that God has placed in your life. Appreciate the things that you wear - your shoes, clothes, jewellery, even your mobile phone. Cherish them, enjoy the features, let go of the past, especially the bad times when you experienced unhappiness. Live for today, for tomorrow you may die.

Have you prepared for it? So enjoy every moment of your life today. Instead of complaining about life, your finances, or a health condition, speak God's word of blessing, speak words of life; those words will go into the realms of the Spirit and produce the change that you want to see. You can speak life into your body, your job, your family, your finances, and even your future; your words carry power, therefore, whatever you want to change, talk to it, will respond.

The poet, Dale Wimbrow, wrote:

The Guy in the Glass

When you get what you want in your struggle for pelf,
And the world makes you King for a day,
Then go to the mirror and look at yourself,
And see what that guy has to say.

For it isn't your Father, or Mother, or Wife,
Who judgement upon you must pass.
The feller whose verdict counts most in your life

Is the guy staring back from the glass.
He's the feller to please, never mind all the rest,
For he's with you clear up to the end,
And you've passed your most dangerous, difficult test
If the guy in the glass is your friend.

You may be like Jack Horner and "chisel" a plum,
And think you're a wonderful guy,
But the man in the glass says you're only a bum
If you can't look him straight in the eye.

You can fool the whole world down the pathway of years,
And get pats on the back as you pass,
But your final reward will be heartaches and tears
If you've cheated the guy in the glass.

During the winter months, plants and trees may be dormant, but they are still very much alive. We, too, may have dormant periods, but we can know that, despite appearances, the life of God is active and powerful in us. We are one with the life of God and we are constantly attuned to God's life and light. What we need to remember is that we are children of God, made in his image.

Even as we affirm life and healing for ourselves, let us send out thoughts of healing to those we know are in need.

In our personal life, we may sometimes feel that we are walking in unknown territory, that the pathway we need to take is obscure. At such a time, we can know that we have our very own personal guide with us to help and guide us. If we are unsure of the pathway to take, Spirit will clarify our thoughts and show us the way that is right and good. We like to think of ourselves as self-sufficient but it's wiser to know when you need help. God's creative silence imparts to us a new sense of direction, a new source of strength and a new level of quiet trust and faith.

In each and every life more opportunities to progress and real benefits are missed than seized. If we fail to grasp them and use them they go, rarely to be recalled and so we fail to grasp the opportunities when they are presented. Life of Earthly span is comparatively short but its fleeting seconds are of much importance and precious to all. Few realise that life on Earth is a testing time; the one and only test by which the standard of entry into a future life will be determined. As in the present sowing, so in justice will future reaping be. The fruits of all your daily actions will be garnered and will themselves praise or condemn when the body is vacated.

So, today, CARPE DIEM - seize the day.

CHANGE

They say that "A change is as good as a rest", but for some people, change is hard; it does not come easily or naturally. We get set in our ways, we have our own opinions, views and ideas about the things that matter to us, some maybe of little consequence, others not. If your life is anything like mine, it will be pretty well planned out; I have a diary to remind me of appointments, meetings and other 'to do' things.

Inevitably, interruptions change my day and while they can be frustrating, sometimes they can be productive and the change of routine takes me to a different place or to meet someone different. I believe that some of the advances in our lives have come through a change or interruption in our normal routine and sometimes it takes courage to challenge our own thinking and to change it.

My mother would always say to the family: "Take your problem to God in prayer, leave your troubles in God's hands and have faith."

Her confidence that her prayers would be answered seemed to reflect her belief that God would bring a change of purpose and direction. Her confidence was evident in the family home. Prayer can at least bring peace and a calming effect on all the family. It can also bring shape and purpose into their lives and to look ahead with confidence with God firmly in view, because it holds promise for this life and for the life to come.

A lot of good can come from the right words, spoken at the right time. One word can change someone's life and help heal hurting hearts. Gracious words are words that are kind and loving, thoughtful and sensitive. We want to express these words towards others, especially to those who need them most.

Sometimes people find themselves in situations that get them discouraged, and as much as they want to believe that things will change, nothing seems to happen and they lose their confidence and enthusiasm to move on. So then is the time to change your frame of mind and influence your words. At that point, whatever radical changes you desire, condition your spirit for success and keep talking that way until your spirit is conditioned to think success.

Make the foundations of your success today, let the Great Spirit be the foundation and anchor of your life. That is what will keep you standing when all else fails and will keep you on the path of success all your life.

Due to the busy life many of us lead, it is not hard to recognise ourselves in overextended situations. Successful people allow their God-given talents and passion to guide them in life. Make the choice to do something because it engages your heart as well as your mind... and let no one change your mind.

There are times in your life when everything you attempt to do seems to go wrong. These are the changing scenes of life. The Great Spirit has a purpose for not allowing you to be fruitful all the time. Real growth requires a season of struggle, as well as a season of success. Your life is like the trees in winter - they struggle loose their coats and then as the season changes, springtime allows them to refurbish their strength and prepare for the next season of fruitfulness. As you look back on your life's accomplishments, you will notice that your Creator has given us a season of sunshine as well as a season of rain. Each changing season serves an important purpose.

You were intended to have a rich, full life within; you are the means to achieve it; you possess all the necessary equipment. God has given you the tools so that you can finish the job. Before you receive anymore, you will be observed with what you have, so don't let your dreams die inside you. Take a chance with your spirit friends who guide you, it just maybe the bridge that gets you where you want to be.

Your life is a mission to discover and comprehend the laws of the Spirit. You can only achieve it by helping others, for the question asked will not be what have you done to enhance your development but what have you done to help your fellow man to fulfil his divine destiny. By helping others your outlook will change, for nothing pays greater spiritual dividends than loving your neighbour, which means acting towards him in the spirit of goodwill.

I know that life in this world can be difficult, and at some point most of us have wondered what is our purpose. My wife has just had a very bad illness and had to be admitted into hospital (a big change to her normal routine), in a room occupied by three other ladies who, after only hours of togetherness, soon became a family, sharing each others troubles and exchanging life's stories. Their illnesses brought love and kindness into fruition; it was as if they had been brought together to help each other through the life-changing illnesses that they were suffering. Although all had different complaints, I think we all gained from the experience of illness.

We have not far to look for signs of a Spirit World, it is discoverable everywhere. We detect it in loving hearts, kind thoughts, gracious sympathy and simple goodwill. All bring the spirit of brotherhood. As I write this, I realise that in a few hours it will be a new year and that I have had the privilege to have seen eighty-three of them. In those years, I can assure you many changes have taken place. I have lived through war and peace and hope that 2015 will bring us a better world to live in.

I wish you all a Happy New Year and send you love and sunshine from Joyce and myself.

A song from the past comes to mind, unfortunately, I cannot recall the name of the singer:

Time may change the secret of the ocean
Time may change the language of devotion
Who knows what fate may have in store for us
Let's make it more for us than ever before
Time may change the colour of the pages
Rearrange the tempo of the ages
These changing years, may disappear from view,
But time won't change my love for you.

Make 2015 the year you change your life. God bless, Sid.

COLOURS AND MUSIC

Having read many books and listened to many good speakers on the subject of colour, I soon realised that music and colour intermingle and it would be true to say that they both play a big part in our lives.

From childhood, parents attract their children with coloured things - Rattles and Plastic rings etc. People are attracted by coloured lights; all the shops and restaurants in the cities have flashing lights, trying to draw our attention towards their establishments. I often think of those people who are colour blind. Could you just for a moment put yourself in their place and imagine when looking at things that they are all of the same colour? I know it would affect me, as I choose my food with my eyes. I once heard my father say: "God bless the man who invented paint." I suppose we could thank God also for the inspiration given to artists and those who paint and decorate in a commercial way, brightening up the world, one could say.

We are all attuned to music and colour, we all have a favourite tune and colour, and we all act differently towards them. You should follow your own intuition as to what is right for you.

To put into words the meaning of spiritual colours is not easy. Most people interpret them much the same. For example:
Purple - Spiritual Wisdom, **Blue** - Healing, **Pink** - Love, **Orange** - Warmth and Wisdom, **Green** - Courage and Healing, **Yellow** - Spiritual Intelligence, **Red** - Power. Combinations of these are interpreted accordingly: **Black** and **Brown** are the colours of the earth; Black reflects no light and should not be present in the aura. We are told not to wear black if we want to progress spiritually and materially. Brown is the colour of earth (basic life). When Brown presents itself in the aura, that person lacks confidence and is tied to material things. Brown, when blended with higher colours, is good, showing a good balance both materially and spiritually.

From the beginning of civilisation, colours have played a big part in the lives of people. In all ancient rituals, e.g. weddings, funerals, christenings and conformations, White is always worn. White symbolises virginity. Men of Religious orders were dark colours, the symbol of humility. It is interesting to note that Black and White are often worn together. Nuns wear a White coif and Friars have a White waist cord. The druids wore White and a vicar wears a White collar and surplice.

The colour signifying Kings, Queens and Emperors is Red and Purple.

Blue, Mauve and Pink, we associate with healing, doctors, nurses and all those connected to the service of healing the sick.

A short survey taken amongst friends shows that most people react the same to colours, e.g. Red to almost everyone relates to danger or anger. Let's look at some other colours: Purple in the aura to everyone meant a person of high wisdom; a strong spiritual power exists around them, so this is the colour to aim for. We have already said it is the colour of Kings, Queens, Noblemen and church leaders.

Blue the healing colour. The healing rays that are used are mainly Blue; it is a colour worn by nurses. Blue is predominant in Spiritualist churches and it is a favourite colour for most people.

Pink is the love colour and very important to have in the aura. Pink signifies a loving nature and is delicate. Develop your spiritual love; there is nothing like it on Earth. An old saying when someone enquires about your health is that "I'm in the Pink."

Yellow, when present in the aura, denotes spiritual wisdom and is the colour of spiritual intelligence. The deeper the yellow, the more highly developed is that person in their Earthly employment. The yellow we seek is the bright Gold, such as the daffodil or the clear Gold of the sun. Yellow is termed as caution.

Orange - warmth and wisdom. People who have Orange in their aura are of a warm nature; one who has concern for others at heart and always ready to lend a shoulder to cry on.

Green is God's colour, the colour of all nature, it is cool and courageous. Green brings healing in Earthly form. Think how soothing it is to the eyes, the sight of rolling hills down to the valley, or trees in the spring with new green leaves. Green is a good colour.

Red is the colour of power, very earthly and in its lower form, aggression; very much of the ego. A warning colour. A colour to distrust if it is blending with the lower colours. Sayings like "the red flag", or "a red rag to a bull", or "I saw red" tend to say Red is anger. Red denotes anger.

White depicts purity, and is of the highest vibrations. It is a power colour and is rarely present on its own in the aura because white attracts and reflects other colours and neutralises them, thus making the dark come lighter.

So we know that colours can assist you in your development and help you to draw the right vibrations. Colours can help you assess the people you meet.

Now we draw together colour and music.

Music and the Effect of Music

The effect of music on a person may be happy or sad. It can bring back memories, and sometimes a happy tune can bring back a sad occasion. Music can take you back in time, to childhood memories, and can bring an instant change of mood.

Music and colours are inseparable and each note in the scale has its own colour. Music brings colour into our lives and many songs have been written about colour, e.g. 'Red Roses for a Blue Lady', 'When the Blue of the Night Meets the Gold of the Day', 'The Green Green Grass of Home' and 'Tie a Yellow Ribbon Round the Old Oak Tree', not forgetting 'There's a Rainbow Round My Shoulder'. The composers must have had a reason to put colour into music.

As the artist sees and paints a picture, composers see music as a picture; music and colour cannot be separated. Also, the effect of music can stir people into action, soldiers into battle and marching. Music can be emotional and touch the heart.

It could be said that every human being is like a note of music; each person has their own keynote and vibrates to it. In the same way their liking for colours differs; blend a group of people together and harmony can be achieved.

Music stirs the emotions. It brings love, power and energies and all represent God. Everything in this world has its own sound, whether it be animal, vegetable or mineral.

Let us conclude with 'Light'. The lights of the body are the eyes; all the experiences of one's life are reflected in the eyes. Doctors and opticians can diagnose conditions of the body by looking into the eyes. I'm sure you have heard it said that people talk with the eyes. Have you ever given someone the eye? Then there are those who are said to have smiling eyes and what about the third eye?

The eyes are the lights of the body and the windows of the soul, and are of different colours.

COLOURS

INTRODUCTION

Putting into words the meaning of spiritual colours is not an easy task. It is easy to remember that there are seven main colours - symbolised by the Rainbow - and from these stem all the tints and hues of nature. The sum total of the Rainbow, or Iris, is the white light, the highest spiritual vibration of all.

People are often attracted by colours that suit their spiritual and physical personalities, hence depressed, nervous people will often wear dark, sombre colours - a good guide for the clairvoyant. While people requiring courage and confidence will wear bold, bright colours, you will often find that spiritual, sensitive people will wear pastel shades, or the higher spiritual colours on which the Spirit World vibrates. If you wish to draw in a certain vibration then you should wear the colour that responds to it. It does work.

Match up the colour to the sound: Red - aggressive, envy in Green, Pink - happy and bubbly, Brown - quite and relaxed. Sound and colour go together; we react to the affect that they have on us.

It is not possible to argue in a room decorated in Pink, because Pink reacts on the muscular system in our bodies and they go slack. The sight tells the muscles and the muscles slacken and it is not possible to build the aggression to argue. This is a scientific experiment that has been proved. Scientists made a person very angry, placed them in a room decorated in Pink and they immediately became calm.

When you go to the dentist and you have your tooth drilled, you feel tense and then you are told to rinse your mouth out. What colour is the water? Pink. Now, I am told that there is not a grain of antiseptic or healing lotion in the water; it's Pink because it relaxes you, it makes your face relax. It is very cleverly thought out. That little Pink pellet that is dropped in the water is purely to relax you.

So you see we react to such things.

It is said that Orange reacts on the brain and that if you slept between Orange sheets they would upset your sleep pattern. Try to purchase Orange bed sheets. I don't think you can.

One story is of a schoolteacher who needed to have time off work and always worried because the head teacher gave her a hard time and grumbled about not being able to cover her class, until one day she noticed that the clothes he wore were always Brown in colour - Brown shoes, suit, tie, everything was Brown. So, the next time she needed to take time off, she arrived at school dressed in a Brown outfit. When she asked the question, the head started to grumble and then she noticed a change in his attitude towards her. He sympathised and said: "Take as much time as you need." Just knowing how to approach his colour code gave her the power to overcome the head teacher.

When you visit a fast food restaurant, take notice what colour the décor is. Usually it will be bright in colour - Orange, Red or White. These colours stimulate the digestive system; they are not relaxing because they do not want you to stay and uncomfortable seating is usually part of this exercise. So, if you have a weight problem you should not have your kitchen decorated Red or Orange because it stimulates the appetite.

When you go to the cinema take notice. When there is a romantic scene, the décor is usually soft Pink. Remember, Pink for happiness and passion.

Purple and Black used for funerals. Purple is the colour of evolution. Why do elderly ladies wear shades of Lilac? Because it goes with their skin and possibly their hair; also, it can be an acknowledgment of wisdom acquired. You cannot lend wisdom, you acquire it, for life. They reflect the wisdom they have learned by wearing the soft Lilac or the evolution of the beautiful Purple.

PURPLE

The colour of achievement. This is the colour of the ribbon the badge of our ministers is suspended on, to show achievement. So, in funerals we use the Purple to say that they have progressed, they have achieved something and we award them with the lovely colour of Purple.

Black is far from being a depressing colour, it is the colour of spiritual darkness (we hide that), much the same as people who are a little overweight wear Black to hide the bumps, because it's slimming and much the same as Black hides the emotions. We can hide inside black.

In much the same way it is opposite to White. White is for a new beginning, hence brides wear White, the beginning of a new way of life, a baby, a new beginning, a clean sheet of paper, a new start - you are starting with a clean sheet (that's an old saying). At school, how many times were you given a new exercise book and thought: "This time I'll keep it clean and tidy and the writing will be perfect?"

A child will always match its colours to their moods (try it) but ask yourself: Does not colour affect you? It affects your aura. The aura is the rainbow of the soul, your own personal rainbow, just as the rainbow arcs the world, is the aura around it.

Each of the colours in your aura gives the different meanings. The Red, Orange, Yellow, Green, Blue, Indigo and Violet are the necessary emotions to make the world go round. The colours you project in your aura tell about you. They show your strengths and your weaknesses, they show, at any given point, the state of your health, they show your feelings and aspirations. They show absolutely everything about you. The aura surrounding you just now may be good but it can change very quickly according to the change within yourself. As you become fed up, so the aura will become duller, so watch it. I'm keeping my eyes on you all!

You may be sitting quietly and everything is lovely and placid and then the telephone rings, or something disturbs you. This will change the colours in the aura. You are composed but if you have bad news or a shock this would show up in the aura. If anyone can see it, because it shows and relates to everything the body responds to. There are very few people who have the gift of being able to see the aura. Those who do, tell us it is like a reflected light around the head and shoulders, like the colours you see reflecting around a street light at night, or the lights on a Christmas tree changing all the time. It changes with your moods, with your strengths and weaknesses, with your feelings of tiredness of the body.

The aura around you now will probably be different in a short time because it is responding all the time to our emotions. Right now, you may feel bright and breezy but in twenty minuets you may be tired and worn out, so the aura would change. Instead of being bright and shining, it will become dull as you become fed up. The aura is affected by everything we do - what we read, eat and feel, your emotions to other people and what you see and hear.

RED

Red in the aura suggests energy, warmth, love and light. It is the blood colour, which gives the body energy. Take some away and the body loses energy, but given a transfusion it is restored. So, when you see a good Red in the aura, we know that person is full of vitality, passion and love. If the Red weakens, we can see the body diminish healthwise. They say that a person showing Red in the aura is prone to anger.

ORANGE

This is an energetic colour; the very sound suggests a person with a magnetic personality. This colour in the aura depicts a person who has strong vitality; a person who puts action into life and helps others to do the same; an organiser, a person with practical capabilities, who will give of their own energies many times without conscious thought, so depleting their own energy levels.

Orange represents a person who has a magnetic personality, a person with charisma, who will give moral support to others and stimulate them with words and actions (often artistic), who can bring life from their thoughts. A person who truly knows how to give freely from self without asking for rewards.

YELLOW

When Yellow is present in the aura, it tells us that this person wishes to learn as much as they possibly can. A person of self-control, who uses logical thinking to reason things out. A person who is in control of their emotions, someone who has developed and spent time in studying higher things and has the courage to find out the truth for themselves instead of relying on hearsay, or the thoughts of others. Someone blessed with knowledge and wisdom.

GREEN

Nature's own colour. We, in this country, are very lucky to be surrounded by all the lovely shades of Green and if you think about it most things we eat start of Green. In my opinion, Green is the main colour. Some say it is the heart colour because it comes in the middle of the rainbow suggesting it is in the heart of the rainbow. Green in the aura tells us the person is a good listener, and should be in the aura of doctors, carers, social workers, people who do counselling and - of course - healers. Green is a healing colour and is the basis of everything. It is the backcloth of nature. So, Green forms an important aspect of our own present and actions in times of stress or calm. It is seen in a person who has the ability to work with others and able to bring into being a harmony by which essential work can be done smoothly.

Copper bangles left to the elements will turn green, back to their Earth colour.

BLUE

There are as many shades of Blue as there is Green. Blue represents the water of life; without it we would die.

People who have Blue in the aura, depending upon the shade, are usually of a spiritual nature. It is the colour of speakers; a person who is able to talk; The Orator. It is the colour worn by the police, who represent law and order, fairness and discipline. It is shown in the aura of people who are much organised, very appreciative and very caring towards humanity and are usually articulate, a person who can be forthright one minute but withdrawn the next, yet truthful and who expect truth and trust from others.

INDIGO

A colour between blue and purple, many people see Indigo differently. It is like that of Navy Blue. I'm sure that you ladies find it very difficult when trying to match this colour. I was with my wife, shopping and a lady was trying to match a top and skirt. The shop assistant said that they were a pair but the lady said one was black and the other Navy Blue. From where I was standing, one looked Navy Blue and the other Purple. We must get them right. But when you see Indigo in the aura, you will know it is not Navy Blue or Purple. it's that beautiful pulsating colour, which is blue with a touch of Red - very intuitive. It is the colour of mediumistic abilities, mediums, that of composed, still people, who have learned to tune into a higher vibration. These people make good healers, who wish to work hand-in-hand with Spirit and are able to communicate with Spirit on such a beautiful level that you are getting towards expectance of purity.

Indigo is seen in those who work hand-in-hand with higher influences, those who give freely, goodwill towards others. Those who have overcome many of life's obstacles.

VIOLET

The colour of spiritual serenity, of progression spiritually, the vibration of harmonising. We are told that people who have Violet in their aura are of a special nature and not many of us achieve this colour. Violet is associated with the crown chakra, it is supposed to have a thousand petals with seventy-two large ones in the centre and is situated on the head where, as a baby, we have a soft spot - "the symbolic open door" through which we communicate with our creator, we are told. That is why monks shave the centre of the head and the artist paints the halo over the head, to depict a highly-evolved holy person.

Well, friends, this is just a starting point. I am sure you realise that colour is a subject we could talk about longer, for we have only touched on the primary colours. Those of you who are mediumistic may be able to understand and interpret colours when you see them.

COMMUNICATION

You cannot command or demand help from the World of Spirit. What you can do is put yourself in the right conditions to receive them and when you have made yourself spiritually ready, the higher power will reach you.

I remember when I was first inspired by Spirit and did not have to worry about preparing a theme for my service; I had faith that my spirit guides would provide me with words of wisdom.

Now, I need to think before I speak, not that I do not trust my spirit helpers but I need to be able to look back and keep a record of the event. I feel very privileged to be able to sit with pen in hand being inspired, sometimes making numerous notes before it finally comes together.

The difference is that when I stood up to speak and allowed Spirit to take over, there was a wonderful feeling throughout my body, but after the event every word was lost, so my way of being inspired today gives me more satisfaction.

All around me are scraps of paper, with just a few words on them, waiting to come together to make a whole. I know that as soon as I get the inspirations I must write them down or they will be lost. This may seem laborious when I know, like a good friend of mine who is a good speaker can, as once I did, stand up and give some wonderful philosophy with the help from her spirit guides. Oh how I wish she would record it.

But, for myself, I retire into a place of silence and wait for my inspirers to bring those words they want me to broadcast.

Communication is a part of everyday living. To obtain spiritual growth and develop, we must work very hard, using the divine love and sincerity, so it would be true to say that we should first try harder to communicate with those who are around us.

I remember, well, asking the children in our church lyceum, how many different ways we could communicate with someone without speaking - answers with the hands, a nod of the head for yes, a shake of the head for no, or a wink with the eye and thumbs up. We all agreed the hands speak best; we can point left or right, up or down, long or short, square shape, round, pear shape and I'm sure a wave of the hand can be understood by people anywhere in the world.

But, just as if you were speaking, it is vital to transmit what you wish to say clearly and at the right time, depending how you receive your information, whether it be spoken or written, you may have to find different ways to interpret and sort out the information given. Always remember that the meaning of message given is the responsibility of the giver and not the receiver.

If the giver of the message has had good training in the understanding of symbols, colours etc., he or she should be able to decode it efficiently and the receiver should be able to understand what has been said.

A medium is an instrument and like all musical instruments, some perform better than the others, so if we want to be used as an instrument then we should strive to be one of the best. Then I'm sure that we would be sought after by the best in the Spirit World.

You are as much a part of God, as god is part of you.

A Russian philosopher, Ivan Ilyin, a tailor by trade and a very good one, sometimes got excited when talking about fabrics. He said to his daughter, Nikolasha: "Look around you, one thread pressed against another, pull one of the threads out and the fabric will be spoiled. If one thread tears or gets weak, the whole piece is no good." The same is with people - The Divine Fabric - Learn to unfold all your faculties - spiritual, mental and physical - until you have reached the maximum growth of your development.

In your pursuit to render service, you should be excellent in your delivery; therefore, it is a greater disservice to others when your act of service, which should benefit them, is rendered shabbily. Understand whatever words are rendered should bring succour to the receiver; the infinite power is waiting to illuminate them.

Communication is God's greatest gift to humanity; it is always available without charge, anywhere, at any time, making no distinctions between colour or creed, language, race or nation.

If you offer yourself as a worker for Spirit, you will be put in touch with those who teach variations of the golden gifts from the

World of Spirit. Knowledge, like truth, is infinite and not even the brightest student knows it all.

If you want progress in your development, you will have to pursue many avenues, for it will not come to you without effort. Life is about giving - the more you give, the more you will receive; the more effort you put into your spiritual development, Spirit will increase theirs threefold.

A meaningful life is one that has significance in the lives of other people, using the gifts God has given to you positively, helping them meet their needs and solve their problems. The Brotherhood of Man should be your guiding principle in life.

Throughout the world there are many who live in daily awareness of the guidance of Spirit. Life is a journey and while on your journey, enjoy your trip, relish every moment.

The natural laws always achieve harmonious results. Think of the artist, with all the primary colours on his pallet. Mix them together, they make different variations, changing into more colours and though there may be many different colours, they always blend together to make a portrait or a country scene. Visit a beautiful garden, see the flowers of different colours and sizes, yet they blend together. Nature plants her pictures. Supreme artistry.

This could never be duplicated by Man. Over the centuries Man has always had a thirst for knowledge to improve his environment and to understand himself and the mysteries of life. The questing mind belongs to the fulfilled person who has no time to be bored or depressed. Knowledge opens the door to achievement. Confidence springs from a thorough understanding of one's subject.

We owe a debt to the great explorers of the world. Explorers in every field, from the discoveries of new continents to the inventors who make life easier and exciting. We are grateful to our pioneers who, through their determination to know and experience, paved the way for us to acquire knowledge from Spirit. There is always something new to discover. Great teachers have left us a legacy in the books written over the years. Leisure hours need never be dull.

Let us have a thirst for knowledge, enriching our own lives with purpose and dedication.

CRYSTALLOGRAPHY

I think we would all agree that the world is full of energy. In our lifetime we have learned that many kinds of precious things are taken from the earth - Coal, Oil, Silver, Iron, Rubies, Tin, Gold, Diamonds and many more, and I am sure you will agree that they are all very strong unless they are subjected to heat. The Earth is a storehouse which is plundered everyday for our pleasure. How they come to be is a study, for each has been formed differently. We all know that the pearl comes from the oyster and starts of as a grain of sand.

In recent years, perhaps with the dawning of the Aquarian age of heightened awareness, interest in crystals and gems and the power they contain has been reawakened all over the world. Individuals and groups are finding these powers can indeed be used for the good of Mankind, particularly in terms of healing.

We have by no means learned all there is to know about crystals and healing; we can only give information on what we have experienced or information received of that which is already known. We are told that crystals and gemstones possess a very special energy, and who knows what discovery may be unearthed by those of you who have learned to work with them.

Once we begin to talk about crystals and healing, we have to realise we're concentrating upon a very special blending of the energies of the actual crystal and the user, so it is important that you handle and feel attracted to it before you make a purchase.

It is said that when you purchase a crystal, it will contain both negative and positive energies and that you will have to remove the negative ones and at the same time convert them into positive ones by your own efforts of will and concentration, for it would be wrong to send them into the world without cleansing. It is also said that every time you use a crystal for healing and let the patient hold it, after the healing is complete, the crystal should be cleansed. In my opinion, the best way to cleanse anything is to give it a good scrub.

When I was thinking about the subject of energies, a programme came on television from America about converting one energy into another; it showed a wind farm in America, the biggest in the world, making electricity. They wanted to extend and make it twice as big, but the noise was already too much as it was impossible to stand near them unless you were wearing earmuffs. So then they showed another way of changing one energy into another; they had acres of land covered with tubes picking up the sun's rays and again making electricity and providing one percent of the states electricity, but it amounted to millions of dollars.

Another way of changing one energy to create another is that, as a boy, my father had a crystal detector, or a crystal radio set. It was a crystal with a piece of copper wire running through it, bringing the sound. So, can we, with crystals, using ourselves, bring about a power for healing?

It is said that you must take time to charge and attune yourself to a crystal, but how many people actually do charge and attune themselves? We are told that crystals can help meditation and also, psychic development and healing. Whichever type of mediumistic abilities are yours, the development can be accelerated by the use of a quartz crystal.

I read that crystals can be used to heal through the chakras, though I realise that not everyone accepts the chakras as a fact, but it is advisable for the user not to rush this process, especially when you reach the brow and crown chakras, for you are opening the door to the World of Spirit and you have to be certain that the door is fully open. Ladies and gentlemen, we must be sensible. While I won't say that it's impossible, the question will be asked: Can you prove it?

Many things we use come from substances that are extracted from the earth, or things that grow from it - Paper from Wood, Crockery from Clay, Tin, Lead, Sulphur, Salt and Crystals... and many more.

Two of the best known crystals that most people know are the Quartz Crystal and Amethyst, followed by the Rose Quartz. There is also the Tiger eye. You can grow your own. The best crystals come from Brazil or Uruguay.

Other experiments using a crystal are dowsing, which can also be fun and crystal gazing through a crystal ball.

DEVELOPMENT

The gifts of the Spirit are many and various and every gift has to be earned by the person wishing to become a medium, working to help other people, and living a good steady life. Improving the character and improving the standard of self-discipline also helps.

A developing medium should try to live a good life and be as true to the Spirit as possible, for this will surely reap the benefits, as it is said that like draws like. The thoughts of a medium should be at a high level and with practice, should become easier.

Trainee mediums are all of different personalities that need to be understood and trained accordingly. Each has a spiritual gift, or gifts, which has to be earned by their own efforts. Such gifts can be acquired in the Spirit and Physical World.

When a spirit worker finds a suitable medium to work with, or a person willing to give themselves as a channel to be used by the spirit helpers, the channel may have more than one gift. The spirit worker will soon realise that Spirit will use them for what is most suitable for them at that time as later on, guides change and the channel or medium will be used differently.

One thing to remember is that the gifts, once given, cannot be taken away by others; they cannot be lost or stolen and they do not decay. You are responsible for the gifts; you may lose them if you ill-use or abuse them.

Spirit is anxious to teach all potential mediums and they realise how difficult it is for you to contact them; they are aware of how much time and effort you put into your development. Patience is also needed, both with yourself and the spirit helpers, because it takes time to build up a rapport between you. This, I am sure, you understand. However, when you have succeeded, what joy and pleasure follows. The more you attune to your helpers the better the communication. After a visit from Spirit, both should feel better and richer in friendship for having done an equal exchange as far as possible.

Have you tested the Spirit? Test it for it will respond; it is the only way to gain confidence in your helpers and they in you.

Please do not imitate other mediums you see working; each and everyone is a separate personality. Your experiences are for you only and it is up to you to share them with others. Everyone is responsible for their own progression; each one of you will have to make your own way up the spiritual ladder. You are the one who will have your work cut out to improve your spiritual make-up.

No medium works the same. I am sure you have noticed the different ways guides work through different mediums. It is necessary for you to listen very carefully to what your guides say or impress upon your mind that there can be no misunderstanding and default of this which causes distress to those who receive the message. Try to be sure of what you give; it is up to you to be correct in the way that you pass on information received. Remember, also, we must never stop developing the gifts.

We must work at attunment. God's gifts are there for working at and there is no easy or short way to this wonderful state of being. Think before you do anything and take notice of the first thought... and work from that. Remember that you need links, for all good messages are linked and should be delivered skilfully.

It is said that practice makes perfect, so think before you speak and take notice of the thoughts you receive. Think once, think twice before you speak, this idea will save you much trouble and muddle. Any kind of machine is a wonderful invention. Some are better than others, some have more functions and mediums are as such.

Spirit helpers are with each one of you, ready to help when asked, but they cannot run your lives, as some of you expect. You have to live this Earthly life and be able to stand alone. Making your way in life is the key to the next phase in your evolution.

Those of the Spirit World who have passed this way have learned their lessons on Earth, so you see how important it is for you to learn and prepare yourselves for the work in Spirit.

Many who watch mediums at work think it is easy. It is not. In some cases, many evaluations may have gone into the preparation of the medium. Years of patient training are given by those in Spirit to obtain good, first class results.

So a medium is a person whose psychic séances are so acute that they can feel the presence of the non-physical world and interpret the information which is passed on to the recipient, or us the people of the Physical World and this is the time when mediumship manifests and this is important. What matters is the way in which the medium responds to the impulsions of the Spirit. The medium reacts by speaking.

The act may be the reaction of inspiration, whether it be clairvoyance, clairaudience, clairsentience, trance, automatic writing, etc. Some mediums are fortunate and may be used in varied ways. Although it usual for one faculty to develop to a higher degree in the working life of a medium, they often pass from one faculty to another as guides change. It is sufficient in the beginning that Spirit can make their influences felt and the sole desire of the medium should be: "May I become more responsive." The motto of a beginner should be: "Teach me thy way o lord."

Mediums should realise the importance their own consciousness plays in the use and development of mediumship. All spirit impulses are interpreted by the medium's consciousness. Good mediumship comes with the illumination of the consciousness, but with the development of the consciousness into a state where it can most readily respond to the wishes of the spirit operator.

Many developing mediums have the idea that they need not be aware of what Spirit are trying to convey. It is a good thing to remember at the beginning of your development that before you can give one word from Spirit, you must develop an awareness. This awareness will become more acute and your cooperation with Spirit will come about when you learn to react more readily to their wishes.

Through the highest awareness, sitters are usually told to sit and relax and quieten the mind. This, we are told, is a difficult feat to perform. As soon as we try to be quiet, all kinds of thoughts come rushing into the mind and try as you will you cannot push them out. I think that this inrush of thought is no different from what happens at other times; the difference is simply that you have become sensitively aware of what your mind is doing. You are now in attunement, your thoughts are now more active.

When you sit in a circle, you are told to quieten the mind. A mistake here is that we tend to believe that it means we have to think of nothing. Surely, if we sit trying to empty the mind - and if it is possible to do so - then the mind would be as an empty cup, with nothing in it to drink.

True mediumship means thinking of something to the exclusion of all other things. Remember the purpose of your sitting. We spoke of links; we are looking for a beginning, the first link to a message.

Most developed mediums work on symbols. A careful record of what is seen must be worked on. Seemingly meaningless symbols may produce the most fantastic messages and therefore it is advisable at first for a developing medium to establish a firm cooperation with one spirit control in the early stages of development.

A person who is developing mediumship is open to many varied entities and remember, there are good and bad in Spirit. The first step is to find your chief control (or doorkeeper). It may appear to you that to have a greater variety of guides will make your mediumship unique or special and guides are easy to come by. We must remember that it is not the person who has guides in great quantities that brings the best evidence.

What we would rather have are fewer guides with better qualities. The status of the communicator is not important. If status was then everyday people would not have much opportunity to be mediums, but God has given everyone the gifts, equally shared by all, rich and poor alike. It is up to the individual to develop their own progression.

A message simply and clearly delivered is often more telling than a long discourse message. For example, the developing medium will give you just what they receive, but a developed medium may elaborate, hence, it is said the best messages are given by people who are just beginning. It would be wise to remember not to allow Spirit to control you when you are alone; you must decide what kind of company you want to keep. It is like choosing a friend on the Earth plane; we have to get to know them and be able to trust them. Remember again, like draws like - the better life we can lead on Earth helps to make better channels for Spirit to work through.

Ask yourself what kind of channel are you looking for.

The best, I am sure. Well Spirit are also looking for the best.

Now we must blend together as a team and seek from Spirit a team who will be in attunment with us as we sit for development.

EXPRESSING ONE'S FEELINGS

Many of us find it difficult to express our feelings; infact, I suppose just as many may ask what the point is. Is it best to keep things to yourself? There are others who may not know what they are feeling and I am sure that most people think that if they express their feelings, such as anger or misery, people would not like it and would reject them.

It is said that the British people tend to be reluctant to express their feelings directly. In comparison, people from some other cultures, for example, countries around the Mediterranean, are more likely to say what they feel, when they feel it.

There are times in our lives when things happen which make big demands on us and we have to adjust. This may cause us to have a depressing feeling of anxiety and stress, so in life it's up to us and while we may be unable to control our circumstances, we can take responsibility for our outlook and it can transform our experience; in fact, everything we do from the heart mindfully - and with love - gives us a feeling of satisfaction.

The best and most beautiful things in the world cannot be seen or touched, they must be felt with the heart, and ever near us, though unseen, the dear immortal spirits tread, for all the boundless universe is life; there are no dead. R. W. Emerson said: "All I have seen teaches me to trust the Creator for all that I have not seen."

My young grandson called to tell me that he had just been for an interview for a position. He said: "I just knew I would get it because, as I entered, I had a feeling this was my chance." I suppose that he also had self-confidence, which is the most attractive quality a person can have. How can anyone see how awesome you are if you cannot see it yourself? If your body language is confident, it sends out a clear message, but if your body language contradicts your words, it sends out confused messages. We have to accept responsibility for our lives. Then you will get where you want to go and nowhere else.

Living life in the moment embraces the fullness of being alive.

Do you, at this moment, think about how far you have travelled on life's journey? Or do you wonder how far you have yet to travel? Well, hang on, life is a journey; you still have to carry on if you want to complete it. When you come to a spiritual understanding of who you are, you can begin to take control, you will feel the atmosphere change and then you will realise that you have reached maturity, which gives you the ability to think and act your feelings within the bounds of dignity. The measure of your maturity is how spiritual you become on the pathway of your life.

I travel back in thought to the first time I had the feeling of love. Believe me, now that I have reached old age, I realise that this love in the heart is the truest and best and greatest treasure to be found. I also realise that most people think that love is physical, but without feelings of respect what is there to distinguish men from beasts? Immature love says: "I love you because I need you." Mature love says: "I need you because I love you." At this moment, I feel the presence of the spirit inspirers, under the leadership of God, the great lover of Mankind.

Many other recollections come back to my mind with the regard to this gift of feelings. As I opened my door on this February morning, I felt the cold, with an added feeling that snow was on its way. I withdrew back to the lovely feeling of warmth as I entered the sitting room, settled down in my favourite armchair. Feeling calm, relaxed and peaceful, I went to sleep.

I am sure that by now you yourselves can bring to mind other words of feeling, such as happiness and could put your thoughts on paper.

My father, who was a Methodist speaker, always told me an Earthly story with a spiritual meaning and so, with this intention in my own mind, I wrote my books to help the developing mediums. I am never afraid of repeating a story which has proved of value to others.

Many who have purchased my books have written to me telling how my brief writings of my own life, have helped them in theirs.

So with love and sunshine, remember the purpose of life is a life of purpose.

FLOWERS AND COLOURS

"If... in thy store there be but left two loaves, sell one and with the dole, buy Hyacinths to feed thy soul" is a quotation by John Greenleaf Whittier. The Chinese proverb says it a little different and reads: "If you have two loaves of bread, sell one and buy a Lily." I suppose we could change the flower for our own favourite bloom, even one of the wild variety. If you remember, it was the lillies of the field that outshone the glory of Solomon.

Flowers help you raise the mind and have great healing properties; they raise the act of meditation to the highest level, to one of real headway spiritually.

Just for a moment think how the poet Wordsworth was inspired when he saw the daffodils. "Beside the lake, beneath the trees, fluttering and dancing in the breeze." But the fact is he saw them time and time again in his memory. He would lie down to relax. He tells us then: "They flash upon that inward eye, which is the bliss of solitude..." I think this is a wonderful description of the memory. The memory is a precious gift which allows us to go back in time and cheer ourselves up by reliving the happiest moments in our lives. You do not have to be special to see lovely things in the mind's eye. Flowers can make you happy or sad, but a flower is beauty itsself. They are of beautiful colours, they emanate sweet scent, they are soft in nature and influence you to be gentle. If there are flowers around, you can sense a calm feeling, for that is how they vibrate towards us.

When I was a young boy, I can remember that it was not unusual to see men with a flower in their lapels; suits were made with a buttonhole in the lapel for that purpose. Sadly, it's only on special occasions that we see men wearing a flower now.

English women are referred to as "English Roses" and we are privileged to be in their company.

I remember the old films of romance, starring Dorothy Lamour, Cyd Charisse, Barbara Stanwyck, Elizabeth Taylor, Margaret Lockwood and Sylvia Sidney. Beautiful blue eyes in the moonlight, with a flower in their hair.

It is said that flowers can speak for you, and you have heard it said: "Say it with flowers", so we send flowers for weddings, birthdays, anniversaries and funerals. They speak for all occasions, happy or sad.

Here we have a few examples of the language of a flower:

The Forget-Me-Not speaks for itself, the Red Rose says: "I love you", the White Rose suggests peace and purity, the Red Carnation, passionate love, "I must see you soon", the Bronze Carnation denotes friendship, the Tiger Lily says: "My love has no bounds", the Mistletoe sends a thousand kisses and of course, Pansy for thoughts. I remember my mother saying that the spelling gives us P-for sincerity, A-for Attentiveness, N-for Neatness, S-sincerity, I-Industry, E-Ernest, S-Self- Sacrifice.

So flowers are a way of speaking to someone and for those of us who are shy, they can be very useful, for they give endless joy to the giver and receiver,

Many famous personalities have made use of flowers to express their feelings. Nero, who was extravagant, displayed his glory by covering the whole surface of Lake Lucile with roses. Just think what a sight that must have been!

Cleopatra, for one of her feasts that she held to honour Anthony, covered the floor of her palace with eighteen inches in depth of sweet smelling rose petals. There's romance for you.

Song 337 in the Spiritualist Lyceum Manual states: "Kind words and sweet smiles are the roses of life." Yes, if only people had roses in their hearts, there would be no more wars, no misery, just goodness and beauty

Give a thought to the Rose, for it is credited with many healing and curing qualities. There are more than thirty remedies compounded from their leaves, not forgetting wine made from the hips and petals. The dew collected from the Rose is said to have healing properties good for the eyes.

I'm sure you know that the White Rose is the emblem of Yorkshire and the Red Rose pepresents Lancashire. The wars of the Roses still continue today. In the past, knights of the realm had to have special permission if they wanted to display a Rose on their shield.

It is said there are over a thousand different varieties of the Rose. Harry Wheatcroft, probably the most celebrated Rose grower, said: "He who grows Roses must have Roses in the heart." The Red Roses of Life. I'm sure, like me, many of you have purchased the artificial Red Rose for the heart foundation charity.

One of the finest stories about the Rose is that surgeons carrying out the most intricate operations on the heart, pin a single Red Rose of Life on the machine that takes over the functions of the heart and lungs while they sew up. The Rose remains within sight of the waking patient to whom it was presented by the theatre sister. At one famous hospital, no operation begins until the ritual has been completed. This is magical psychology. Think what it must mean to the waking patient to encounter such beauty when they come round after the operation.

Enough about the Rose, let's think about the little Snowdrops. I think everyone waits for them to appear, for they herald the coming of springtime and after a cold winter, they bring brightness into our lives. Snowdrops have a Floromatic name; they are called Lights of the Earth and said to bring good fortune.

There are flowers that tell you the time of day - the Pansies open at sunrise and close at sunset, and before gardeners could afford watches, they took their time from the flowers. They took special notice of the Sweet Sisters or Copper Cups, to warn them it was midday and time for a break. The Star of Bethlehem was nicknamed Lady Eleven O'clock because it opens at eleven. Marigolds go to sleep at 4pm and Water Lilies at teatime. Night Scented Stock open at about 8pm and close at daybreak... and many more.

Nations are known by the flowers - Holland, the Tulip, America or the USA, the Rose, England, the Sweet Pea, Japan, the Chrysanthemum, Wales, the Daffodil, Scotland, the Thistle. And just as nations are known by their flowers, so are many human beings. Is there anyone here today named after a flower?

Maybe sometimes you feel like a Rose in a bed of nettles and we know that the nettle has a sting and maybe you have been stung in the garden of life, but remember the nettle can be useful; it can be eaten as nourishment, it can be made into a drink and it can be used to alleviate pain. Everything is useful in the gardener's world.

What your Valentine Bloom depicts:

Anemone = Love Sick
Pink Carnations = Woman's Love
Red Chrysanthemums = I Love You
Daisies = Innocence
Yellow Iris = Flame of Love
Jasmine = Sensuality
Mimosa = Secret Love
Sweet Pea = Farewell Au Renoir
Red Tulips = Declaration of Love

The colour Peach often signifies romance while Red and Orange symbolises passion.

Today, an arrangement of flowers are sent in a sponge with water to keep the flowers alive longer.

God is like a sponge to us, a constant power and love and we can draw on that source at anytime.

HAVING A PURPOSE

Without an aim or purpose in life, we become like a boat without a sail, drifting through life, taking whatever comes our way, whether we want or not. Then, when we take control of our lives and find a purpose in them, however small, we find that life has a meaning.

In these times when we do manage to get busy with some purpose, we find how amazingly our health improves. There is no doubt about it, faith, or belief in Spirit, will bring an improved condition. Give yourself to Spirit and you will never regret it. If you have not felt a change in your life, remember, like the raw diamonds which have to be cut and polished to bring the best in them, so do human beings and very often this takes time and is sometimes painful.

We all begin our Earthly life aggressive, selfish and thoughtless and gradually, over a period of incarnations, we learn the lessons of tolerance and compassion.

To use an old fashioned word 'sins' committed by us some time in our past lives have to be paid for; all our misdeeds have to be corrected in order to permit spiritual progress. You may say how terrible to suffer such a fate but, for me, it's a better fate than being cast into the fires of hell, as other religions would have us believe.

A lesson learned, however harsh, advances us along the path and sometimes the harsher the conditions the further we advance. Everything has a price, nothing is free, this is one way to find and develop your life's purpose.

A bad action exacts its return! Charles Kingsley said: "Do noble deeds, not dream them all day long." Our task on Earth is to progress. The dictionary defines Progression as "an act of moving forward" but in spiritual terms it means much more. It means a transformation within yourselves. You look for the truth in everything, you are more aware that you see things that you would in the past have closed your eyes to, your thoughts are more active.

This mental state of reaching out gives access to the influence of spiritual forces through which we are all strengthened. These are some of the many ways to find and develop your life's purpose.

To be at one in God is to be aware of His directions at all times and at all levels of understanding. If you cannot accept God in the smaller things, you cannot expect to find Him in the larger ones. To acknowledge this with every waking thought and deed should become so much part of our daily lives that it should be as natural as breathing. It may seem tiresome having at all times to cultivate good thoughts to be truthful but the purpose of this life is to live it, to taste experience to the utmost, to reach out without fear and find newer and richer experiences. You were put on this Earth to achieve your greatest self, to live out your purpose and do it courageously.

You were put on this Earth to contribute in some way to make things better. My father was a philosopher and had what he called his "theory of purpose", which held that everything in life has a purpose, that God created everything for humans to enjoy - food, drink etc. but not to abuse. "Everything in moderation" was his prescription for a life of purpose.

HEALING

I am sure that you will agree with me that no human being can claim to be a healer, but we can offer ourselves as a healing channel for the spirit guides to work through, and yet we are proud, as humans, to be called healers. Having a clear understanding, we can now use the term 'healer' for the person who is acting as the channel.

The average healer claims that all that is necessary is for the hands of the healer to be placed on the particular part of the body causing the trouble and the healing power will flow through and achieve the required results. If this so, that healing power must come from a divine force through certain people who have been chosen as a channel for this work, then you might agree that it is the source that matters and not the instruments, but the instrument or healer lends their support and amazing cures have been affected.

There is no doubt that spiritual healing is becoming an important factor; the evidence is seen at every healing service and the miracle of healing is being revealed.

Sadly, the great gift of healing is being neglected because we do not try to improve ourselves. The medical world does not stand still; investigations are being carried out continually, so we, as healers, should try to improve not only the quality of healing but an advancement into psychic surgery. We could also include a course in counselling. The Chinese believe that one way to heal is to be a good listener. I'm sure that listening to someone who has troubles would be of great value. We should talk with the patients and explain that they must not expect to be cured instantly. Instant healing has been known, but usually the benefit is experienced over a period of time.

The healer has to encourage the patient to have a positive outlook towards the healing process, building up a rapport between healer and patient so that the patient is able to relax and allow the spirit healing guides to bring the healing power and transfer it through us.

The easiest way of finding out what is wrong with the patient is to ask them, but the basic method used by the healer is to pass their hands over the patient's body and when the fingers find the affected spot, clairvoyantly, as some are, receive the impression from their healing guide. Others, who are not clairvoyant, may feel a tingling sensation running through the fingertips.

Others, who are considered to have the special gift of being able to see the aura. The aura is made up of colours encircling the body; just like a rainbow, each colour represents our make-up.

The story told by the aura is fascinating to those who can see them; they can diagnose the health of a person by the blending of the colours.

Most healers concentrate on the hand method, that is centreing the hands on the afflicted part of the body through their normal clothing. Patients I have spoken to tell me that they have experienced heat coming from the healer's hands, heat which penetrates even though some were wearing thick clothing. This is because in most cases heat rays are used; however, occasionally a cold sensation would be felt. In some different cures, this could be as a negative and positive approach.

It may be necessary at some time to have two healers to lend themselves together for the benefit of the patient. My own feelings are that at all times, if possible, healing should be performed by two healers, preferably one male and one female.

Sometimes a patient may fail to benefit under a certain healer; perhaps a change of healer would achieve results. A watchful eye must be kept in this direction as some healers tend to specialise in certain ailments. This, I believe, is because we are chosen as an instrument by workers from the Spirit World, so a certain healer may have been attached to a doctor or specialist who has passed over. This would make the healer a specialist and would account for particular success with individual ailments.

A healer needs to be a born humanitarian, have a big fund of sympathy and humour and also a practical knowledge of the physical body. We know that certain healers use colours in their diagnosing of a patients illness; it is realised that certain colours are used for particular complaints. Let me assure you that this colour healing is a fact, as I remember my father always wore a platted blue silk neckband to keep him free from a throat infection and swore that red flannel on the chest helped with lung complaints. So, these colours would be seen in the areas of the body by one who is sufficiently sensitive to colours.

There are many searching questions that men and women constantly ask, that science, philosophy or any great organised religion can answer, such as: What is the purpose of life? Why do innocent people have to suffer while the guilty sometimes appear to escape all punishment? Why is there so much injustice in the world? Why if there is a God of love, does he allow cruelty and war? Why is Man allowed to inflict pain and suffering on others? To give you answers would be above my mission. All I can do is to try to help you to have faith, capable of sustaining the heart and satisfying the reason for a way of life that will prove itself, so that we can make our lives luminous and beautiful. I believe being a Spiritualist fulfils these needs.

I also believe that healing is the highest service a man can render. Our teachings are spiritual and we all must try to unfold that spiritual self from within us.

Some scientists go as far as to admit that there is a sort of power current in every human being, and strangely enough this force exists in every living thing - animal, plant and even mineral. They tell us that this energy force is used in Spiritualist healing. This force can be transmitted from man to man, from man to animal and from man to mineral and visa versa. Gardeners transmit this force to their plants and they flourish such that the gardeners are spoken of as having 'green fingers' and maybe you have experienced the magic of crystal healing, so this force, which is found in every living thing, can be transmitted back to man to heal his own ailments and so, it might be said, that spiritual healing has a scientific background.

We are paddling on the foreshore of spiritual healing; some results we cannot explain but we know they happen and we must, therefore, accept the fact that they are true. Spiritual healing is the greatest gift that God bestows on Man and is certainly the most spiritual one. The reason why healers give so willingly of their time and service for other people who are sick in one way or another is because they posses divine attributes of love and compassion for those who are in misery and pain and they yearn to be part of that great force which restores them to health and happiness.

We must look a little deeper into the science of healing. To understand energies, we must first study the composition of matter itself. I read in a science book that all physical matter is composed of atoms and each atom is a form of characterised energy. Each element is constructed in an identical way and when one form of atomic energy is associated with another, it produces a third substance. To explain: For example, when lemonade is mixed with beer, it weakens it and produces a third substance called a shandy.

When the healer and the patient blend together with the spirit guide, a change is brought about - an easement to the part of the body being healed.

To bring a change in the existing state of specified matter, additional energies have to be applied to it; for example, we apply heat energy to boil a pan of water. Under spiritual healing, when arthritic deposits disperse, it must follow that some other energy had to be applied to them to induce a chemical change in their structure and bring about their dispersal. Arthritis is medically incurable; medical science has not yet been able to discover any form of treatment to dissolve the crippling adhesion. Scientists are now able to split the atom, change its structure and break up the characterised energies that comprise it.

The healing guides do the same, but with their advanced wisdom and knowledge of spirit-formed energies and their physical counterpart, they are able to direct to the patient's joints energies that have the qualities of inducing a chemical change in the state of the deposits, thus splitting the atoms comprising the arthritic adhesions.

It is contended that our hands possess no healing qualities. We use our hands to express the healing intention. For example, if a patient has a pain and we seek easement for it then our hands will move in a soothing movement as if to take it away. The hands express the intention of the healer; they are indeed the servants of the mind, as if our brain is in the fingertips.

It is difficult to imagine any other activity where the intimacy between the hands and the mind is stronger than in the act of healing. We must understand that every healing is a planned act, needing intelligent application, thus, when we ask for healing for a patient, the hands become part of the healing intention to sooth away pain.

To begin healing, we first take hold of the hands; this is more in the way of a greeting, an introduction between the healer, the guide and the patient. I am sure you now realise that the healing power is more easily transferred through the hands.

Spiritual healing is a gift from God. The healer has a great responsibility to be a clean, alert and intelligent instrument which Spirit can work through, free from envy, jealousy, malice and pride - If we do this, through the channel will flow the pure healing water from that crystal fountain that we all love. "They must never in the heart abide."

At all times we must remember that we are humble, dedicating ourselves to the service of Mankind through the love of God. In this way, we will feel the fulfilment within our hearts. It is important for me to treat my patients as my own family; I need to feel that love and understanding. I know that this does help if you can feel as one's own family.

HOW LUCKY WE ARE

I'm sure you, like me, have looked back on your life and said: "If only I had done this or that, my life would have been different."

In each and every life more opportunities to progress and real benefits are missed than seized. We look back and realise how unaware we were of things around us and they pass us by, never again to be recalled. We say to ourselves: "Next time I'll watch out, I will be ready, I will not miss out," but we soon forget or even notice, for things that appear at the time seem so trivial and they pass us by. We realise again that we are the foolish ones. We should be ever watchful for that which may be of great value, but, remember, do not cast aside the small things, for they may be the seeds of great growth.

One of the greatest misconceptions of Mankind is in placing faith only in things that we can see. We forget that unseen forces of unlimited power have been discovered and tapped into for the benefit of Mankind. There is much on Earth of no visible substance but of great worth and benefit to the human race. Everything that has been created in this world are but determinations of unseen thoughts.

Man would, indeed, be helpless if he had sight alone, and if all realities were visible, he would need no other material sense than vision, whereby we see the flowers in all their glory, but none, however skilful, can see or handle the perfume so lavishly given free, melodies sweet and soothing to the ear approach unseen.

Yet who can doubt their existence? Warmth and coldness, bitterness and sweetness are there to be experienced, but like many other sensations of nature, existing also are other realities of a finer degree, which surround all and influence the lives of all, but none are in material form, to be grasped and visibly examined. They are, however, vital and greater in their power for good or bad as love, kindness, cheerfulness, brutality, fear and hate; these all minister to the higher self, as in, like manner, others supply the needs of our bodily senses.

So, now we realise there is much the eye can never see. Where stands he amidst such an array of invisible realities and silent essences to affirm that solidity is the only proof of presence and being? For we cannot see the perfume of a flower, yet we know it exists. To Spiritualists, much that is void of form and visible substance is known to be of great worth and their lives are continually being enriched from invisible sources. The light of understanding is being revealed to them, for many have lived in total ignorance and darkness and now have seen the truth and light. To their great joy, much that has been of doubt and burdened with anxiety has rolled away, leaving a clear unshadowing view of the great wisdom surrounding all things and they rejoice that they have found a new way of life and would that others share the secret of their happiness upon entering into a new world of wonder and delight.

This new discovery, that spirit friends are ever near to guide and sustain their steps through life, knowing that death is a myth, being but natural, that the pomp and power of worldly possessions is a fleeting shadow and not to be compared to the least of treasures to be obtained in the progress of the higher self. Material things are for our passing needs, but spiritual ones are for our permanent good. It is very foolish to build up our aims and careers on shifting sands, for our life-building structure will surely, sooner or later, collapse. The aim in this life is to build something we can take through the veil of so-called 'death', otherwise our Earthly journey has been wasted. How many realise this?

So, carry on and perform your Earthly duties well, but it is wise to cultivate those lofty ideals at the same time. Our material life and our spiritual life must progress together. This is your testing time, to prove your worth. You should avoid handicapping yourself for there are many stumbling blocks on your journey of life. There will always be different degrees of social status but we are all born into this world to breathe the same air and receive the same warmth of the sun, and we are all equally favoured by nature's bountiful blessings. But these are worldly gifts and have no part in our spiritual development. Let us not forget that we can all develop our gifts, regardless of wealth or position.

We all enter this world empty-handed and by earning and acquiring the gifts of the Spirit, we will determine our congenial surroundings when we leave this sphere of activity, as empty as we arrived. We can only take with us our personality and experiences.

The great question will be: How have you developed during your period of life on Earth? We may ask: How can it help us? It gives us a knowledge of the many unseen forces which surround us and ways to benefit from them. It offers the best to all who seek and does not disappoint. Its knowledge is infinitely more important than any Earthly wisdom. It embraces all nationalities and the best points of all religions. It enables the poorest to prepare and arrive on the 'Other Side' qualified for an exceedingly happy life, and it will prevent the millionaire from arriving bankrupt.

It provides all believers with a season ticket to eternal joy and access to unlimited realms of fascination and study. Spiritualism outrivals all other creeds and beliefs, giving proof of its verity and it welcomes all tests. It dates from the beginning of time and will have no end.

JUST A THOUGHT

If Spiritualism appeals to someone, we can assume that their religion has not proclaimed and practised its faith with sufficient convictions, so it's up to us as Spiritualists to continue to give the public proof, but we must never stop striving to better our religion. We are now attracting younger thinking people, who have a more open mind about life and death and yet scientists still probe and try to be obstructive. Scientists cannot explain why a field mouse seals up its home before the bad weather comes, they cannot explain why sheep move to the lee side of a mountain before a storm, nor can they explain how the homing pigeon finds its way home when taken hundreds of miles away from its own loft.

And yet scientists want to investigate our religion, so Spiritualism must stand up to scientific questioning because it is human nature that man will continue to probe. But we cannot dismiss honest investigators, because they want proof before they will believe and who knows, it might be worthwhile, the results could strengthen our religion, but if they cannot find the answer to the homing pigeon then I don't think they will be able to deliver a certain verdict on this, our religion.

Man is hungry for a better world; every continent is rushing hither and thither in a quest for a formula to solve its economic and political problems, forgetting that the world needs a spiritual revival. One perfect formula is that of the golden rule: Do unto others as you would have them do to you.

The crying need of today is not for a change of head but a change of heart. There is not a lack of ideas amongst us but a lack of good will. The Bible story of the prodigal son has a personal meaning to everyone because when people have done their worst with their lives, they want to go homeward to their Father God knowing that he will meet them, comfort them and revive them. His unbroken promise of love.

Your task in this world is to assist those in need of spiritual help. Those who are strong should give their strength and support to uphold the weak. Those of you who have experience should become guides to the inexperienced. Those who have been comforted should carry comfort to the sorrowing. A true worker for Spirit is one quite confident in the presence of any duty. Courage has been defined as "A spiritual quality that enables one to remain poised and centred in God. The realisation that the almighty God of the universe is a spiritual presence which is constantly striving to express in and through us fills us with new courage and a fearlessness that is beyond description."

This is the world of extrasensory perception, ESP as it is popular known, but it has been blocked off from us by our conditioning for decades. We have been taught that what is 'real' is only what our five senses perceive. Scientists say that ESP has a future whereby we can be in instant touch with others around the world, hurdle time and space with a leap of the mind, know the future, the past and the present and cure our ills through the power of the mind.

And yet ESP is controversial. It is an open invitation to charlatans who pray on confused and eager seekers and yet on the other hand, clairvoyants are being used by the police. They are also used to find water and minerals. In America, archaeologists, using a medium to direct them in an area, dug up deeply buried treasure, so we could say that ESP is replacing the spade as the archaeologist's primary tool. In health work, psychic healing has become commonplace and been accepted by the National Health Service, something to be desired.

Spiritualism is being looked at; it is becoming more of a reality. The brave pioneers of the past survived jeers and contempt, knowing that the fruits of their labours rested on sure foundations and so we have developed, from the early stages to the present day, on a path prepared for us. It is up to us as to what we achieve.

The hymn, 'Breathe on me, Breath of God', comes to mind. Words we often sing but maybe without thinking a great deal about their meaning. But if you do, you will find there is a great power in this breathing in of life; it is the first thing the physical body does when it is born into this world and the last thing we do when we take our last breath and leave it to return to the Spirit World. We should breathe in the love of God, which is the life of this universe. You will live forever in this universal life.

And when you do leave this world, you will not cease to breathe, for life goes on exactly the same as before; you continue to live and breathe whether in a physical body or a finer matter. You leave your Earthly body and then pass into a finer ether and at an appointed time - return again to Earth.

How wonderful it is to have breathed forth from the heart of God, for man is a composite being and when the time is right, is born into this world. But being a spark which comes from God, we could term ourselves as "Children of God" and as we grow in this world, we are still linked with our creator and when we are in need or in trouble can link in prayer and ask for help.

Some people are afraid of death; we don't want to leave our loved ones but, my friends, in the process of rebirth into the Spirit Realms, you will be united with all your loved ones who have gone before you. And where there is love, there can be no separation, for love is like a magnet to steel. The question we must ask ourselves is: Are we prepared for our death?

Life begins at death, though I am dead
Grieve not for me with tears
Think not of death, with sorrow and fears

I am so near that every tear you shed
Touches and tortures me
Though you think me dead

But when you laugh, and sing glad delights
My soul lifts upward, to the light
Laugh and be glad, for all that life is giving

Though I am dead, I will share your joy in living

Unknown author

What we must do is move forward in harmony and love, to attune ourselves to the highest level we can reach. We must put behind us all thoughts of care and anxiety and allow our souls to return to their creator and then we shall be known for what we are.

We can change our thinking as we enter into a new world of thought. We may regard these as inspired thoughts, but do not long for some heavenly place of a serene and peaceful Garden of Eden because God's peace is here, it has never left you. His peace is with you always; you do not have to wait until the conditions in your life are in order to experience peace.

JUST FOR A MOMENT

What if I told you that the Spiritualist Movement was a philosophy two thousand years before Christ and that Plato and Socrates decreed that man was a spiritual being and should live his life as a spiritual being? Spiritualism teaches man to live his material life for the betterment for his own spiritual entity contained within him; a spark from the divine.

We must also realise that Spiritualism, in addition to being a religious movement, is also a study movement with a system of philosophy. As to what Spiritualism is, it is the product of the minds of those who searched for and found the truth, it is the key stone upon which lays a deeper aspect of man's relationship to God and our moral relationship to each other.

Spiritualism is the science of life. So what does this mean to imply? It means that life is expressed through the operating laws of life. Now what does this law of life mean? It means that everything pertaining to life evolves through evolution; the evidence to support this is an observable fact that can be demonstrated.

Steiner said: "The evolution of man has consisted in the gradual incarnation of a spiritual being into a material body. It has been a true 'descent' of man from a spiritual world into a world of matter." Now begins this Earthly life, a life which needs to gain experience spiritually, which extends to all facets of a personal life. We Spiritualists know that our primary objective is to prove the survival of the human personality after death.

It is one thing to sense a presence that is entirely outside of one's own life, a presence that guides and inspires us, through clouds and sunshine, sorrow, laughter and tears, but there is a personal experience between the spirit helpers and oneself; they enjoy a definite spiritual fellowship. This spiritual unfoldment is the process by which a person may become more aware of their spiritual nature.

When we think of our beloved dead, we make a mental image of them as we knew them on Earth. Of course, we all know that the body dies and the spirit survives and yet we get near to Spirit through mental images of physical forms that were near and dear to us. We judge the inner life not to be sufficiently aware and so may blot out the presence of our spirit friends.

The great unseen have stores of valuable and desirable information to bestow, so seekers must be earnest in their development and seek only the highest and they will receive the highest to communicate with. This inner change means that everything touching life may be assimilated into spiritual power; the inner change is fundamentally a change in moral tendency.

When we have a telephone conversation, we speak and we listen and in our relationship with Spirit, we should speak less as listening should be the primary importance. They are the givers and the medium is the recorder who speaks what is said to the recipient; a trio working in harmony, each and all have the precious gift of sensing. When man takes a plunge into the future and allows their spirit guides to co-operate with them and the unseen forces which exercise a new and powerful influence upon them, working together to bring those messages of love to one in need and comfort, they have now become sharers in a large resource and comprehensive programme. They have come together to be in tune with the infinite. Sometimes you will be called upon to take part in something you never dreamed of doing. It may be to undertake a new special task which you thought you could never achieve, but to be influenced by the Spirit, all things are possible.

Consider your mind as a garden, to grow and obtain an array of flowers to enchant and delight. To do this, it is necessary to have good soil, but remember weeds also would grow and flourish and spoil the beauty which you are trying to create. Thoughts are the flowers of the mind, so we must cultivate the garden of the mind and let your presence be felt as the fragrance of flowers. Do not envelope in gloom so shall your influence be remembered, for this is how you will be remembered, far longer than the span of Earthly life.

The world's seen and unseen are not so far apart as generally believed. On Earth there are many pleasures to enjoy; however, the choicest garden harbours many things that damage and spoil its beauty. This also relates to life's garden; all our days are not passed in sunshine and happiness, the ills of the body are there to mar our pathway. Those who pass from this world and worthily enter their portion in heaven's garden will find that the many joys that await them far exceed anything the Earth can offer in charm or desire. The progress and happiness of this Earthly life depends on how we co-operate with the Spirit World. Until this is realised and acknowledged and brought into being, there cannot be love, peace and happiness, or a life of everlasting joy for humans of all colours and creeds, progressing together as the Great Spirit intended.

Here, I include hymn no. 177 from the Spiritualists' National Union Hymn Book. A lovely hymn. I wish that I could find the author:

There's a land of fadeless beauty,
Bright beyond the narrow sea;
Where the rainbow lasts forever,
And the stars eternal be.
Homes no human hands can fashion,
There forever shall endure,
Spirit free from earthly passion,
Deathless spirits, glad and pure.

There's a land where chilly Winter
Never spreads its frosty gloom,
Where no deadly blight can wither
Gardens of perennial bloom.
'Tis a land where never sorrow
Bids the mourner's tears to flow,
Where no frowning dark tomorrow
Ever dawns on human on human woe.

Yet in all my finest fancy
Never rose so fair a dream
As this land beyond the waters
Doth to eyes celestial seem;
Where in love's embraces folden
I my cherished friends shall see;
O, this clime so glorious, golden,
Holds a happy home for me.

Those who obey the law of their creator fill their own lives with much happiness. In doing so, they are enriched by love and sympathy they expend by receiving a welcome from those around them, and when they do wake in their new life, the welcome that awaits them ten times richer, will be their reward for all the good deeds and kindness which has gone before.

LIFE

What is life? I was told at an early age that life is what you make it and that this life is a period of time in which we, as individuals, should try to progress. The things that we experience should be as a lesson to be learnt. So we could say life is a teacher.

In life, we experience love, anger, sadness and also joy and happiness. We also feel pain and disappointment, yet God, in his wisdom, gave each one of us the ability to deal with life's problems and if we had any difficulty, we could always take it to him in prayer.

We are told that we learn by our mistakes. I sometimes wonder if this is true as some people never seem to improve their lives. It is said that he who lives to serve glorifies living, he who loves lives to purify himself in living, so whatever path you choose, remember always, that it lies within you to accomplish all things. Don't let your background, your preconceived ideas, your present difficulties, your past failures, your self-doubts, or the opinions of others, keep you from becoming all God wants you to be. The potential that lies within us is limitless and largely untapped.

Cultivate nobility of mind and spirit and greatness will pervade you. Nothing pays greater spiritual dividends than helping your fellow man. Your outlook will change, your mind will become more alert, your confidence will be enhanced. Take gentleness and kindliness with you always, yet be fair-minded. Trouble not yourself with littleness, be large in understanding, live as you would write a fair page in a fine book, or a song of rare beauty.

Life means far more than many of us ever dreamed of. It is not merely passing through this Earth life with all the comforts, enough food to sustain the body and clothes to keep us warm. Life on Earth means that we should strive to bring into our lives the God-like image. We need never be anxious about our tasks in life, for every common walk of life is glorified with God's presence.

The purpose of life from the Spiritualist point of view is to seek from within, to discover the inner self and to be true to thyself. All the happiness and success in life will come as a result of the discovery of the divinity within. You may say: "Ok, if we can enjoy such things, we'll do it, we will find the true self within", but friends, you must be careful what you say because you have to change your whole chain of thoughts and by changing your thoughts you will be on a higher consciousness than many of your friends and you may lose friendships by finding His divine guidance.

By allowing the God-self within to play a larger part in our lives, the spiritual side of our lives will begin to develop. So, it follows that our thoughts are our prime importance. The discipline of the mind is not an easy accomplishment for any of us, although the rewards for such attainment are many. Peace, harmony and the ability to control our lives brings much satisfaction.

We must have the persistence and determination to succeed in order to attain the greatest results; however, with the highly developed will to achieve, all things are possible. All you have to do is provide a vehicle for the expression of the divine self from within; ask God to love through you.

If you want to know God's plans for you, do God's will each day. If there is a large task or some other duty to perform, He will lead you to it. The hardest school tasks are easily mastered in comparison with the lessons of patience, calm temper, humility, unselfishness, forgiveness and contentment. Even at our best we learn these lessons slowly, but as time goes by you can make progress.

Life is not a journey to the grave but into eternity. Our Earthly body maybe totally worn out but when disposed of it will reveal the real person that you are. Think maturely and spiritual growth will suddenly happen. Someone once said that we are not human beings trying to have spiritual experiences but spiritual beings trying to have human experiences. The life force within came from God, who is Spirit, so it's like going back to the beginning and reconnecting with Him. But first you must understand life's purpose and that way you will know what you must sacrifice. The question is, are you going to make choices that bring you closer to your goal, or take you further away from it?

We can start now by loving ourselves. That might seem selfish, but in loving ourselves and our fellow man we begin to love that which our world can give us freely and lovingly appreciate more and more of those things we take for granted, the things we fail to notice and fail to understand. Are we willing to forget what you have done for other people and remember what other people have done for you? Ignore what the world owes you and think what you owe the world. Your duty is to see that your fellow men are just as real as you. Try to look behind their faces and into their hearts. Remember, your existence in this life is not what you are doing to get out of life, but what you are giving to life.

The spirit of God works through the instruments of human society and we, the instruments, are taught by the Divine Spirit, so we are employed by the Greater Spirit. We, as instruments, are contracted to speak the word of God. A responsible task, would you not agree? We are all taught by experiences and observations and I still believe in direct inspiration. Though we may not know how, it is a source of great joy, for it is the Spirit working in and through us. God is pleased to reach down to you the knowledge of the truth. Why? Because you need it? No, because it's in his nature to be generous and give it freely.

Most of life's successes are based on the principle of trial and error, it is said. It's a mistake to suppose that people succeed through success; they often succeed through failure. Sometimes we are doing better spiritually than we think we are, so always be mindful of your manhood (or) womanhood, yet may the virtues of tenderness and peace be yours.

Though I Am Dead

Though I am dead, grieve not for me with tears,
Think not of death with sorrow and fears
I am so near that every tear you shed
Touches and tortures me though you think me dead
But when you sing and laugh in glad delight
My soul is uplifted to the light
Laugh and be glad for all that life is giving
And I, though dead, will share your joy in living.

Author unknown

LOOKING BACK

This year, I have watched the Gladioli at the bottom of my garden. I planted them four years ago and they were planted to cover the fence. Every passing year they have degenerated and this year they are not very good at all; infact, a good gardener would have pulled them out long ago. The leaves look very anaemic, they should be dead; infact, one or two are, but the others have fought their way through four winters, survived the cold winds and snow and struggled to produce a rather pathetic show and yet they don't seem so bad if we take into account the struggle that they have had to produce their blooms. I have not helped as I have not done my part to help them over the year, so I have to admit that they have done their best under bad circumstances and have put on a very brave show.

When I look at them they remind me of people around me. Life, for some, has been hard in one way or another; they could say that they have not had a real chance and everything seems to be against them and yet, like the Gladioli they have struggled through, surviving against all odds. What amazes me is not that people are so bad, but, things being as they are, so good.

As I look at conditions across the world, at the wickedness and ugliness, I realise that we must help, for if we don't they will be like my gladioli in a very short time.

Still on the garden theme, I was looking at the Pansies; the little faces looking up at me. They were beautiful. I remember my mother saying that the spelling of the name "Pansies" gives us: Patience, Attentiveness, Neatness, Sincerity, Earnestness, Self-sacrifice. This gave me a new respect for the humble little flower.

My favourite poem is 'The Daffodils' by Wordsworth. The Daffodils he wrote about grew beside Ullswater in the Lake District but the fact is he saw them time and time again in his memory. He would lie down to relax, to gaze "upon that inward eye, which is the bliss of solitude." I think it is a wonderful description of the memory. The memory is a special gift, it allows us to go back in time and cheer ourselves up by reliving the happiest moments in our lives. You do not have to be special to see things in the mind's eye.

I found these poems and I am sure you will agree they say everything. Unfortunately I cannot find the authors.

MEMORY

Funny thing the memory, a conjuror id says
As though it seems as I look back, to things of yesterday
For half the sorrows are forgot, and I remember best
The sunshine lighting up my road, the times when I've been blessed
The ill is lost, the good remains, and the worst is left behind
And all life's precious little joy's, have nested in my mind.

****

Seeing with unseen eyes
Memories where the picture lies
Looking backwards down the years
Kaleidoscope of joy through tears
Locked within the heart until
At some small word or thought they spill
And floods the mind like waking dreams
Of things achieved and might have been
But as we ponder soon we find
The good live on bad times are left behind,
And with God's help at last we banish sorrow
And learn to face with faith each new tomorrow.

MEDITATION

Today, let us say a prayer for those who need healing. If you know or are praying for someone who seems very much in need of healing, remember that you do not have to pray alone; prayers for healing are offered by healers across the country every day.

Your prayers are strengthened and reinforced as you pray for others to be healed. When you say a prayer for healing, you are serving as a channel through which God's healing work can be done. Through your faith, through your prayers, you are a healing channel. Keep your faith centered in the realisation that healing is the will of God. You must pray for healing confidently, knowing that with God all things are possible.

Let Us Now Feel The Presence Of God's Healing Power

Ask Him to allow you to be a healing channel of His love and feel the power permeating through you. We must co-operate with the healing power and feel the restoring, uplifting, energising activity of God working through you. Know that the true source of healing is the all powerful spiritual healing and that this power works through channels or healers... and all caring people.

What we must do now is to sit quietly in prayer and meditation, to experience the relaxing renewing inflow of spiritual peace, and power, through meditation you can feel the loving presence of God, feel his peace sweeping through you, setting you free from pent up emotions, let us now ask God to come into our meditation, and dedicate this short time, to his good purpose, and ask that we will all be blessed.

In Your Meditation, Be At Peace - Peace With The Infinite

As we leave our meditation, we ask our heavenly Father to guide us in all that we say and all that we do and through His loving direction, through His guiding light and inspiration, we can make ourselves receptive and receive a constant inflow of divine ideals.

We ask that all sick people will receive His healing and rejoice in the infinite possibilities of life. To know that we have placed ourselves in His presence gives us strength and a will to carry on.

"Gracious Spirit, we believe that there is power in united prayer and we ask that our prayers for those who need healing will receive your richest blessing and we pray for peace in the world and with all religious people, but most of all, peace in all human hearts. AMEN."

MEDIUMS

I remember my father telling stories about a workmate called Jimmy Largent. He said that as they were walking to work, this man could put his hand in a hedge and when he pulled it out he would have a bird sitting calmly on his fingers. Years later, I was privileged, through my father, to get to know him. He was a gifted medium and was supposed to be able to produce evidence using a crystal ball, something that at that time I did not understand, but gradually became interested in. After a lot of banter, saying to this man that it was not true, one day, I had a conversation with him and he set me a challenge, saying: "If you dare, come to this address on Saturday night and then you can see for yourself."

I looked at the address, it was in Leeds. I thanked him, saying that I would be there. When Saturday came, I wondered just what I had let myself in for, but after all the hard times that I had put him through, I knew that I must fulfil my commitment, so I went.

On arriving at a very large stone house, I knocked on the imposing front door; it was opened by a tall well-dressed man. Explaining that I was here to join Mr Largent, I was ushered into a very large drawing room, there were about fifteen people present. Seating me in between Mr and Mrs Largent, I was then introduced as the son of a very good friend, who was a disbeliever and - with their permission - would like to have the crystal ball first. All agreed. So here I was, lost, bothered and bewildered. I was given a piece of black velvet in the palm of my left hand and then the crystal ball and was instructed to look right into it. I felt a shudder all through my body. After a few moments, I was amazed as I could see a little girl in a polka dot frock. The question was asked: "Can you see anything?" I replied that I could and was asked to tell the others what I could see, so I described a little girl with golden hair and the blue polka dot frock. A scream of joy came from a lady on the right of me: "That's my daughter; she was killed in a car accident wearing that frock."

I passed the crystall ball to her and her husband, who were overjoyed. The crystal ball was passed from person to person with everyone seeing wonderful things. Still a little unsure at what had taken place, I was asked: "What do you think now?" With a shrug of my shoulders, I said: "Seeing is believing." Mr Largent then said: "Bendigo says to give him the crystal again." Bendigo was his spirit guide. I was given the crystal and told to ask mentally for something to appear in it and in this way there could be no doubts. I thought for a moment, then looked into the crystal and low and behold, there was my blue butterfly, fluttering its wings.

This was the moment of truth, for I had to admit that that was what I had asked to see. The crystal was passed all around for everyone to experience what had happened, which brought the evening to a successful end and for me a new found friend.

Many times I paid him a visit and one day my friend and I went to the church to hear him speak. At the end of the service, which had been an exemplary one, he said that (Bendigo) his guide had just informed him that there would only be one more crystal service and that the friend who was with me could choose the venue. He chose Wakefield SNU Church in Peterson Road.

The church was full with many who could not be seated; the service was out of this world and will never be forgotten by all who attended. Sadly, not long afterwards, Mr Largent fell ill and passed to Spirit. He was a humble man, with a wonderful gift.

Another gifted person who I had the privilege to work with was a gentleman from Huddersfield named Mr Calver. He was a trance medium and healer. The first time that I met him was outside Wakefield SNU Church with his sister. He was in a wheelchair and the church, at that time, had no ramp. To enter, five high steps had to be navigated. The difficulty was that this gentleman was rather corpulent. As he sat in his chair, we were told that we would have to lift him and the chair into the church. Smiling, he lifted the blanket and said: "You can only lift half of me." Both his legs had been amputated! Despite this, he was a very joyful person.

During his service, one could feel the energies emanating around him as he demonstrated his gift. I visited him at his home and enjoyed some wonderful experiences. Sadly, nine months later he passed away.

Queenie Nixon was rated as the best ever transfiguration medium. She was also a very good trance medium. Having the privilege to chair her demonstrations on several occasions, I realised that she was a special lady; the evidence given was always one hundred percent. As I have said, this lady was considered to be the best transfiguration medium, placing her above all others.

The best service of Queenie's that I witnessed was a trance demonstration and was performed in the late Autumn so that when the service started it was still daylight, but as day began to change to night and we realised that we could not turn on the lights for fear that we would cause some kind of injury to her, we could only watch as she ran around the room not once did she stumble. Talk about spirit guidance. This was proof beyond doubt.

Miss Bott was another loveable character, a trance medium of great esteem. When speaking, she had a lovely soft voice, well spoken, but when taken over and Doctor Jim came through, it was awesome; from a soft spoken lady, now a booming voice of Gentleman Doctor Jim.

If you had already attended one of her services, you would wait for her to look around the congregation and low and behold, anyone who was sitting with crossed legs would be told with sternness to "Uncross your legs." Everyone had to be totally relaxed.

Mrs Jeans, a lady with plenty of bodily weight was one of the best clairvoyants at the time, always precise and always allowed her black girl child, who she called Topsy, to take her over. Many times I felt the power coming from her. I admired this lady for her dedication, as she travelled many miles by bus and rail. Rain or shine, we were never let down.

I suppose that there are many people who knew the late President of the Spiritualists' National Union, Gordon Higginson. Many knew him better and more intimately than I but, still, the short time that I spent in his presence was always special and enlightening. He was unique. Gordon travelled thousands of miles, lecturing, giving clairvoyance and performing physical phenomenon demonstrations. To say his mediumship was out of this world is an understatement. If you were ever to be lucky enough to be present at one of his transfiguration demonstrations, I can tell you it would be something that you would never forget. The charisma of this man was something to behold. A hard working president, performing all the official duties of a minister, heavily involved in the financial business of the Spiritualists' National Union and his great passion was the Arthur Findlay College, or Stansted Hall.

Horace Wright was secretary of Wakefield Spiritualist Church for some forty years. He and his wife, Florence, affectionately known as "Flo", worked hard to build the now existing church in Peterson Road. Flo held coffee mornings to raise the £200 needed to buy the land it now stands on.

Horace was a gifted medium but his special talent was psychometry. People were asked to place an object, photograph, or something special (if possible, only they had handled it) in an envelope, given a number from a book of raffle tickets and the envelope was then placed in a box.

Always starting with a prayer, then Horace would take an envelope and give a reading. The envelope was not opened until he concluded the message and then only by the person who had the corresponding number, who would confirm if the reading was correct. Not very often did he get it wrong. Many times he would describe in every detail the person in a photograph and what they were wearing. Sometimes it would be a favourite place that they had visited with the person in Spirit. He would describe it accurately.

On one occasion, he took one of the envelopes and threw it on the floor, stating that whoever it belonged to would have to explain their actions to him if they wanted to retrieve it. Nobody did. Afterwards, we all were waiting to see if he would open the envelope and he did, in the presence of the church committee. To our amazement, in it was a ten shilling note; this had been handled many times and was owned by someone who had tried to ruin the service. All I can say is that he was guided by the Spirit.

Mrs Clara Sharp, a Bradford medium and another well-built person was a very popular medium. It was always exciting when she was on the platform. A very fast speaking person, you would have to listen very carefully or you would miss what had been said, as she never paused. I remember receiving a message from her, bringing a string of sausages: "You know what these are, bangers, just like the car that you intend to buy. Ask about the exhaust, they will tell you a story, but it will be two cheeks without a nose. Another car will be offered to you in a strange way." How right she was!

Mrs Dyson, a well sought after clairvoyant from Brierley, South Yorkshire. She would not call herself a medium, as she was a very popular at private readings. I was introduced to her in 1970 and called to see her whenever I was passing her home. The last time I sat with her was at her daughter's home as she was not too well, but the message she gave me was so precise and gave me evidence that saved me lots of heartache.

Mrs Hilda Baraclough, again from Brierley, South Yorkshire, with her sister, Lily Hobson and her husband, Matt, was responsible for the building of Brierley Spiritualist Church.

Mrs Baraclough, a gifted medium, demonstrated her gift, leading the open circle on Friday nights for many years, always to a full church, even today.

Mrs Mee, from Perston, a Geordie, was a very good medium, travelling all around the British Isles. The evidence she gave was outstanding. Her demonstrations were always well attended.

Mrs Alice Deaton, another good Yorkshire medium, whose dress appearance was superb. Wearing a two-piece costume and a large hat to match, she stood out in a crowd. Her mediumship took her many miles in times when the law was persecuting Spiritualists, working with other outstanding mediums such as the famous Helen Duncan.

MEDIUMSHIP

Mediumship is for proving life after death, and depends on strong enough factual evidence to convince us that our relations and friends exist in another dimension - heaven, paradise, or whatever we choose to call it, and that indeed we can - and shall - encounter them again.

Plenty of evidence exists, although different people give different valuations to it. The first function of mediumship is to provide evidence as to the reality of a spiritual universe, peopled by those who once lived on this Earth. You should not take this for granted and you should be able to prove it for yourself.

Your task is to prove survival, your function is to bring a closer association between people of these two worlds. A question asked is: Where does religion figure in mediumship? It is felt that the purer the individual's life, that mediumship of the highest and purest form is the result. Mediumship is to encourage the physical expression of love and compassion at all levels.

If our mediums are to be selected from ordinary people, it follows that we should, in every possible way, do all in our power to raise the standard of the common man. Many people find the way to ESP experiences on their own, thus providing their own direct evidence.

As a result of their experiences, the communicator has reached some altered state of consciousness, which is difficult to understand within their present way of thinking. What has happened is a change in one's nature. It is now beyond dispute that the unconscious mind finds ways of telling us things which have lain within our nature without our being aware of them.

Difficulty arises when the beginner needs to describe what has been seen and if they have no idea of how to understand the difficulty of the symbolic language they may have to interpret, it will be extremely difficult for the communicator to describe these as they really are. More attention will now be given to the study of spiritual laws and to exploring the inner side of the subject. If we are looking for good mediumship, we must also have an appreciative audience for it, then we have to teach people the existence and value of the life in the body of the Spirit. Spirit within and without.

When you become aware of what I can only describe as an "harmonious atonement" around you, or a beautiful divine power and such indescribable joy, then you will know that you are in tune with the infinite power. The work of the Spiritualist extends far beyond the walls of a church or psychic centre, it embraces every aspect of life. We are servants of humanity; you and I represent the church and religion. People look at us and say that we are Spiritualists. We are known for what we are. If you want to be a healer or a medium, the price is not cheap, you will have to be dedicated, because so many people depend on you. Your time which is precious, is taken by others. Are you prepared to give and not to count the cost?

As a medium, you have a great responsibility to the message receiver. Messages must not disturb or perplex. We must bring comfort to the ones who mourn, give hope to the faint-hearted and strength to the weary, then your part in the scheme will have been worthwhile. Mediums have a mission to perform; they have to learn to sift the wheat from the chaff and the facts from the myths to find that which is the truth.

The power of the Spirit inspired those in days gone by and gave them a vision, enthusiasm, and a desire to serve. That same power is available to you. God gives it to you freely, to 'use', but demands that we say nothing that is not given by the divine intelligences. Show in your life that the power of the Spirit is in you, and works through you. The task of the teacher is to make you understand the responsibilities that you have to others.

Through your mediumship, you can bring happiness where there is unhappiness, knowledge where there was ignorance, and when all seems at an end, we can bring hope and then at least we have been of service. Those who have the knowledge of Spiritualism have something that is precious; you have a priceless knowledge of the truth, that you are a part of the Great Spirit, that you have learned to respond to the vibrations of the messenger that the Great Spirit has sent to watch over you.

If the Spirit does survive and wants to make contact, how else can they do it except through the limited instrument of the human being still on Earth? One of the vital functions of Spiritualism is to make available to men and women the knowledge of spiritual life. Such knowledge, if rightly used, could give birth to a higher morality. Knowledge must come alight and burn its way through the walls and barriers of wrong ideas and ignorance and superstition which some members of the public accuse us of. Spiritualism, coupled with its principals, could bring into this world a higher morality in politics, science, religion and philosophy. Purified and enriched by this knowledge Spiritualism could bring many new benefits in every direction of human life.

The presentation of mediumship will need to change and so will the people who are the recipients. I have said that we need a people-based religion, but sadly most people who attend our church meetings do not want to listen to an address or philosophy, most are message seekerss. So our task is to educate the message seeker. It's nice to have a message now and again, otherwise mediums would not be needed, but the more we attend our church, the less we need a message as we become more aware of everything around us, and we draw strength from within.

Mediumship of real value demands a discipline which is far more than merely putting out one's best efforts whilst actually working. This means the constant stilling and refining of the mind, the refusing of the constant distractions in our lives, the ability to remain uncorrupted by importance and petty power, by flattery, money or illusion of self-importance. True mediumship requires the removal of anything which stands in the way of serious communication. Your work is to give that which has a purpose, to demonstrate the existence of the Spirit, and spread the knowledge given. Show in your life the attributes from Spirit because the power of the Spirit is in you. So, retire into the silence, forget this world of problems, tune in to the delicate vibrations of the spirit life around you and live in the light of spiritual freedom.

Remember, each and every one of us are unique; there is no one just like you and you must develop your own characteristics, not copy other mediums. A mistake that many developing mediums make is to be pushed onto the rostrum too soon. This can be detrimental. The word 'preparation' comes in here. If we have decided to sit in a development circle, first of all we have to ask ourselves: What is the purpose of our sitting - clairvoyance, trance, philosophy? You must realise that mediums of the future must prepare for his or her labours, just like any other worker must do, for the people who employ you want better standards. There is a lot of ground work to be done before you become experienced.

The ideal conductor for a developing circle is a fully developed medium, someone who has experienced the pitfalls of the rostrum. How can anyone who has never experienced the pitfalls, or done platform work, help others to overcome them?

A good medium who leads the circle is a person who does not use the power created to give messages themselves. If they do then they selfishly take the power from the sitters or developing mediums. The true teacher will never stand as an interpreter for another, but will endeavour to bring from the one who they are teaching a true knowledge of himself that they can become their own interpreter.

Always open and close in prayer, take it in turns, it's good practice for everyone.

MEMORIES

For the past six or seven years, my wife Joyce and I have seen the old year out and the New Year in at our local hotel. We sat in the same seats as last year, and we were joined by the same people who sat with us on New Year's Eve in 1991. A remark was passed was that "It is as if we have been here all the time." As if time had stood still. We all agreed that time does not go by slowly anymore and that we get older without realising what is happening to us.

We all had plenty to say about our younger days: "Those were the golden days, never to come again." "What cricketers there were in those days, such strokes and such mighty hits." "No footballer could distribute the ball as in our days; to play the game one had to be tough, we had a leather ball to head, not one of these plastic ones."

"The old actors, well they could act, the films today have no stories to tell" and yes, we were sitting in what was once the church vicarage, now a hotel. Our friends remembered the vicar who lived there; he could preach a good sermon. If only we could hear sermons like his again. I am sure no one would begrudge us our golden memories, glowing more and more colourful as we came to the bewitching hour. A new year comes. What lies ahead? There is an old saying that "the future never lies ahead of us, but creeps up on us from behind."

The essential truth of this is the fact that we always make our future before we live it. The problems of today are not the products of today; they represent the thoughts and choices of yesterday.

So, we awaken the sleep memories of the past and come across the incident that left so deep a mark upon us. We look back and wonder what the new year will provide for us.

No sooner had we wished each other a "Happy New Year," when the news flashed across the across the world: Another person killed in Ireland, fighting continued in Yugoslavia. Nothing had changed.

Then it comes down to this. Amongst things that may happen at any moment on any day, there may lurk something that is marked with destiny. Our chances of happiness and usefulness in the future come and peep at us; they take us unaware when we are off guard.

I do wish, at this season of the year, when we go around buying expensive things, everyone would stop for a moment and think of the many others who are fighting for a mere existence. Life for most of us is of very mixed experiences; it includes rainy days as well as sunny days. Love, laughter, and labour are in it, so are sorrow and pain. Unless we have known all these things and more, can we say we have lived?

Love And Sunshine And A Happy New Year

These short inspirations were written between 1990 - 1999 and published in the Spiritualists' National Union, North Yorkshire District Council's, magazine, 'Link Up,' under the heading, 'What's Cooking?':

Over the past week I have come across several definitions of, Spiritualism.

One said: "Spiritualism is not a religion, it is revelation, a positive source of teaching, which may exalt man to a higher understanding of truth and a purer worship and adoration of God." Another read: "Spiritualism is not a religion but a magnificent profession of truth, which carries all the responsibilities of religion."

In the book 'The Arcana of Spiritualism' by Hudson Tuttle, it says: "Spiritualism has no creed, for it cannot formulate a dogmatic system. It is the science of life, here and hereafter and is founded on facts. It regards belief without evidence as valueless."

Another definition says that "Spiritualism is not a religion; it is the discovery of an actual fact in nature. Like other facts in nature, it has always existed and operated, even before it was discovered. It did not come into being just because it was discovered, any more than the continent of America came into being just because Columbus discovered it."

90

I also came across the statement that "Spiritualism is a movement which differs from all others, for it began without a leader. It came into being under unusual circumstances simultaneously in different parts of the world. Abnormal manifestations of more or less identical nature occurred, which provoked attention, simulated investigations and the result spread far and wide."

The Spiritualist philosophy is of great importance. If followed, it will bestow countless blessings on those who practise it. We have a lot to live up to in our way of life to realise how important our religion is; to accept responsibility. The greatest danger to the Spiritualist movement comes from those who speak for thrills, or for self-gain.

We have been given a wonderful jewel to take care of and we must not allow it to become tarnished or lose its brilliance. Let us all pull together to advance and make our presence felt, remembering that we are members of a spirit-guided movement.

Those who believe there is life after the death of the physical body and that life is a an infinite prolongation and evolution of this know that the spirit remains unchanged in being and changes only in conditions where it may hold communications with those in this life who are Spiritualists.

Here is a book of chapters three
The past, the present and the yet to be
The past we know, is put away
The present were living, day by day
But the third and the last of these chapters three
Are in gods hands,
He holds the key.

Anon.

Goethe, the German poet, said: "It is far better to lead your life as if there is a God, when perhaps there isn't, than to lead it as if there isn't, and then find there is."

"To tell the truth, runs the gauntlet of criticisms, abuse and attack.
"Worrying about death, once it happens, you can forget about it."

How many times have you heard the saying: "Think Positive?" We are told that we must at all times think positive thoughts and those thoughts are living things.

This is not something new, for this phrase is used in every book that has been written on personal development. It goes back to ancient writings and can be found in the scriptures of the Bible in one form or another. So why is it that we all need to be told time and time again to order our thoughts? I suppose the answer is quite simple: Most of us have not yet mastered the thought process we engage in every moment of our lives.

James Allen wrote: "As a man thinketh in his heart, so is he." We must realise that we all are, at this moment, greeting our future by the fabric of our thoughts. We can transform the lives of those around us by the thoughts we send in their direction, so take a good look at your thinking pattern and ask yourself how positive and beneficial your thinking is. Are the thoughts you create supportive of life? Do your thoughts uplift and inspire you to do better things? Remember, thoughts create feelings; therefore, the way you feel is determined by the way you think.

One of the most important changes we can make is to start loving ourselves. That might seem selfish but in loving ourselves, and our fellow man, we begin to love that which our world can give us freely and lovingly, and we can appreciate more and more of the things we take for granted; the things we fail to notice and fail to understand. Are you willing to forget what you have done for other people and remember what people have done for you? Can you ignore what the world owes you and think what you owe the world? Remember, there are no superhumans. Successful people are those who have developed a strong belief in themselves through a positive way of thinking.

The episode of Earth life is the force of great value, in developing character, in enlarging knowledge, in cultivating new friendships and generally adding to the richness of life.

Yesterday, I went to fill the kettle. I turned on the tap and no water came out. What a surprise! When the water is turned off, even for just a short time, we quickly clamour for the restoration of that precious fluid. I cannot remember how many times during that short period I went to the tap only to be disappointed. I said: "I wish we had a well in the garden" and if we think of a well, we usually think of a deep hole in the ground containing water.

The history of many countries of the world contains many references to wells, and the great importance of life. The well was the public meeting place. I experienced this as a boy visiting relatives who lived in a Norfolk village. The only supply of water was from the well; here people met and exchanged thoughts and feelings. In days gone by, when local tribes were in conflict, the natural target was the well. This was poisoned and usually brought quick submission from those residing there. I could enumerate the blessings of water in many ways - it keeps us alive and it cleanses the body. Every one of us is likened to the well; it produces pure water unless someone puts poison into it or stirs up the mud within it. We can only draw from the well of self what we allow to be drawn from us, so it is up to each and everyone to ensure that only pure thoughts and feelings are extracted when we go to this immortal well which holds, sustains and brings forth everything which is ever created.

Every human life is a force in this world; on every side our influences pours perpetually. If our lives are true and good, this influence is a blessing to other lives and we should never forget our joys are just as much required by the Great Spirit which charges the well with great love for our benefit. Spread the joys you receive from the well of life, for we must get our lives so attached to God so that we can draw from his fullness in time of need ("God moves in a mysterious way, His wonders to perform").

I feel privileged to have been born at a time when everything seems to have happened. I have seen the telephone come into most people's homes, the washtub exchanged for a washing machine, we have vacuum cleaners instead of carpet sweepers, and the radio. As a boy, on Saturday afternoons, we met at the home of one of the villagers to watch television. This new invention was wonderful. Since then, we now have calculators, computers, fax machines and now the internet. Oh, I forgot, man has walked on the moon, we have jet planes that travel faster than sound and most people own a motor car. What a wonderful world!

I have just answered a knock on the door; the little boy from next door wants to know if I want a pizza. "Just pretend," he said. I gave him my order and away he went on his tricycle. Two minutes later he returned with my pretend pizza, he pretended to take my money and gave me my pretend change. I remember when boys played engines and engine drivers but things change. The phrase "when I win the pools" has now changed to "when I win the lottery."

And we expect everything in an instant - instant coffee, instant custard and meals in the microwave oven. We are continually devising and making new, improved products to make things faster and to perform better (We live in a press button existence).

I suppose it's true to say that, with all these new inventions, we should have time on our hands, but I hear people say they have no time to spare. Whose fault is that? We should take control of our lives. These new things, good as they may be, need some of our time. The TV controls us, the car needs our attention, newspapers need reading, and the telephone always ring when you are giving your time to something else. I suppose people today are busier than ever before. There are more things competing for our time and energy. To keep abreast of time is an insuperable task for most of us. Life surely does not consist of doing more things faster and in less time. Must we not ask ourselves: What is the final end of all this?

I suppose that we shall go so fast that we shall meet ourselves coming back and end up in a whirlwind!

I must go now as my little friend is back. Can I mend his puncture? So, some things do remain the same.

I have just found this limerick called 'Relativity' by Arthur Henry Reginald Buller:

There was a young lady named Bright,
Whose speed was far faster than light;
She started one day
In a relative way,
And returned on the previous night.

This morning, I visited my sister and her husband. They are Salvationists and both have played in the band for many years. But now that the years have caught up with them, they need all their breath to get around. But they have their memories on tapes. They listen to themselves playing. As I entered, I was greeted with the hymn 'Through All the Changing Scenes of Life'. I suppose people of my age and older could say that we have seen more changes than any other generation. Change is something we cannot avoid and many times we do not agree, but we have to accept the change and adapt.

We cannot expect that things will always remain the same, but amid changing conditions and circumstances in our world, or in our individual lives and affairs, amid changing attitudes and opinions, we can be assured of a changeless source of light and understanding. The unchanging wisdom of God is always with us to reveal the right ways. Truth is unchanging; hold fast to your truth and do not fear other changes, or resist them. If we flow along with the good, we will grow along with the good.

This magazine was a quarterly one, so it gave those people, who contributed, the opportunity to write about the different seasons, so I will put my renderings in the next chapter.

PHENOMENON

Today, we are going to discuss physical phenomenon.

I think it would be true to say, that not everyone is convinced that recorded happenings of the past were correct or true.

So many fraudulent mediums were discovered, prosecuted and jailed. This then held back experiments looking into this subject.

The first time that I heard the word physical phenomenon was a long time ago, when I was very young. I heard a lady in church ask another: "Are you going to the physical phenomenon on Wednesday?" I was wondering what she was talking about. So, after a little while, I plucked up enough courage and asked her what it was. My face went red as she shouted across the room to her friend: "He wants to know what it is." Her friend answered: "Bring him with you."

The next Wednesday arrived, the weather was very cold and in the afternoon it started to snow. Getting ready to go, Mother said: "Where are you going on a night like this?" I must explain my mother and father were staunch Christians. I evaded her questions by saying that I was going to a church meeting, said cheerio and left.

The snow was now settling, and by the time that I arrived at the bus station all public transport was running late. My new found friend arrived saying: "Should we go?" But at that moment a bus came, so off we went. The journey was slow, we arrived late. My friend knocked on the door, we were greeted with: "Hurry we are just starting." We rushed into the hall, put our coats on hooks, my friend gave me her gloves to hold andwe went into the sitting room. A lovely coal fire greeted us. There was a round table in the middle of the room with four chairs placed around it, on the table was a large school type bell and two small glass ones.

I sat on the opposite side of the room from my friend, putting her gloves under my chair. The conditions were a dim lit room with lovely fire light. After a cold journey I could have quite easily gone to sleep. Four ladies filled the chairs, placing their hands on the table and within a short time it began to move, and the bells began to ring, not loud, but so that we all could hear them. Then the table leaned right over, but the bells remained as if stuck. The bells were removed and the table left the ground some three feet into the air.

All done, lights on, tea served, and then a lady came over to me and told me that I was greatly blessed, as she had seen a cat under my chair all night. I kept my secret!

Many people have, and still are, relating stories of physical phenomena, and it is said that two of the greatest men in this field was Sir William Crooks and his associate a Mr D. Home then there was Florence Cook and Kate King.

In a book written by Crooks, he tells of Home making a wire basket, putting in it a piano accordion and placing it under the table. Then, the sitters placed their hands on the table and the accordion played a tune.

A few years ago, I was told of a circle where a heavy table elevated up to the ceiling; can you believe it? If you saw it, would you say it was genuine, or say seeing is believing? If I could, with the help of the Spirit, put my finger through a piece of wood would you believe it? And if you brought someone to see it, what do think they would say?

Now, this tells me that Spiritualism could not depend on physical phenomena for its survival. Spiritualism and it's future, I feel, depends on the clairsentients and healers.

What is happening here is nothing to do with the religious philosophy of Spiritualism. I would not like to think people outside would believe that is what Spiritualism is.

My own Philosophy is, test the Spirit, it will respond.

So, we have to keep on experimenting until we get it right and prove it without being called a fraud.

Always remember, modern Spiritualism is in the light.

PRAYER

Usually, anyone who feels that life is meaningless and without purpose often turns to prayer.

Prayer helps to establish a person's faith and strengthens the will to find a meaning in life. I establish justice in my life through prayer. I pray first that God will understand me and I ask for His guidance. I include others in my prayers, and if a situation seems unjust, I pray that everyone involved will find his or her perfect fulfilment. I pray for everyone to have understanding and guidance that everyone will work together to bring harmony into the world.

I thank God for this moment before me. I give thanks for yesterday, I bless tomorrow, but live for today.

Friends, thank God for all that you are, for there are many less fortunate than we are. Those who are sick in body, mind and spirit. Those who live in countries with governments who dictate and oppress freedom. There are many millions suffering hunger. They may be separated by distance but prayer brings us closer.

I breathe a prayer of thanks that God's healing power is at work and that healing takes place, and if one's life needs direction and purpose, I know that God's spirit can be trusted to make plain the way. And I know that the guiding light of Spirit is always shining always, revealing the right path.

So, we pray for our loved ones; those who are unhappy that they can, through prayer, establish faith in God and find a new meaning in life.

As we pray for self, for love and for direction, new, advance openings come, the productivity of our nature opens up along with new thoughts about life and our part in it. Then, prayer by prayer, we can transform the pattern of our lives.

We know that God is the spirit of wisdom and if we would take time each day to acknowledge the Great Spirit and quietly listen to its directions, we would emerge from our prayers relaxed and refreshed. Taking a few moments now and then brings our thoughts, feelings and emotions under control. We know that thoughts are living things and we must have order in our thoughts. With the power of prayer, we are able to quell anxious thoughts and feelings and bring a calm peace within us.

So, in prayer, we place ourselves and all our longings in God's care. We turn our lives over to Him and let His spirit move through us, inspiring and directing us.

There is another form of prayer, which consists of repeating a certain form of words, which sometimes becomes meaningless. Now, I say without any hesitation that every prayer is heard by God. We pray from the heart, something of the basic essence of our self goes into it. God's inspiration flows to all human beings who make themselves available to receive it.

God wants a voice in this world; He longs to express himself to the people of this world. He calls for channels of expression, for men and women who will continue His work. We expect God to listen to our prayers and to answer them, but in our asking we fail to listen to the needs of God, and when He gives us our desires through prayer, do we think how can we repay him? And you know, everything we need or use in this world has to be paid for? So then why should we not repay God for what he has done for us, with interest?

People simply regard prayer as a way to ask, beg and plead. We think of prayer as a one-way system in that if we ask earnestly and persistently and long enough, God will surely respond to our cry.

So what about our relationship with God? That is a question which we are inclined to shirk. Surely we need to build up a closer relationship, and through prayer, God does not remain a stranger for long. Knowing that we have the God spirit within us, the spirit of wisdom, we have a centre of peace to which we can always return.

So, in prayer, we place ourselves and all our desires and longings in God's care. What really matters now is that we find some way of praying that is real; we do not want time-wasting prayers, for we are all troubled by wandering thoughts. We must forget selfish prayers that begin: "Please God, give me" and say: "Make me, show me and use me."

For it is in prayer that we ask for renewed trust and stronger faith, for more tolerance and love, especially to those who differ from ourselves.

I, myself, have always found prayer difficult; so often it seems like a fruitless game of hide and seek. I Know that God is very patient with me. Without that patience, I would be lost. Yet I cannot leave prayer alone for long; my needs drive me to prayer.

There is a story of two sailing ship captains stranded in port, waiting for a good, strong wind to start their voyage home. That night, on retiring, they both sent out prayers asking God for his help. One asked for a south wind, the other for an easterly wind, both had good reasons. Now, God had to decide. You know that one of them will not get his prayers answered, but God, in his wisdom, knows everyone's needs and if he cannot answer your prayers, he will share your suffering.

Mahatma Gandhi said that he could do without food for many days, but could not do without prayer for one.

God Answers Prayer

I know not by what method rare,
But this I know, God answers prayer.
I know that he has given his Word,
Which tells me prayer is always heard
And will be answered soon or late
And so I pray and calmly wait.
I know not if the blessing sought
Will come in just the way I thought
But leave my prayer with him alone
Whose will is wiser than my own
Assured that he will grant my quest
Or send some answer far more blessed.

Eliza M.Hickok

PROVING A POINT

A book that I am reading states that there is no need to quote examples of hymns through which we can express our thankfulness to God.

My opinion here differs with the authors. I feel an understanding of the SNU Hymn Book can and will prove to you and I that hymns can speak to our emotions, our imaginations, our consciences, our wills. People have been truly inspired by Spirit to bring and join words of wisdom and music together, and just as words and music inspire the congregation, bringing them closer together as they sing out praises to God.

We realise that some of our hymn writers were neither ministers nor professional poets, but ordinary people, who loved to sing and write.

One of my father's favourite hymns was 'Trust and Obey' and I know those words meant so much to him in daily life and in his religion, and just like the author, I got to know most of the great hymns of the church on Sundays, as my two sisters and I were given a choice whether to attend the chapel with Dad or go to the Salvation Army with Mum. At the age of fourteen, I deserted them both and joined the local church choir. As a young boy, I must admit that singing in the choir was very painful when all my friends were playing football, but in later life hymn singing became very important, a very important resource for my personal worship. Now a minister and prison chaplain, I am thankful that I can memorise so many hymns from other religions. At an early age, I could join with many a congregation and enjoy a service of song. Now an octogenarian, they never leave my subconscious mind.

Let us now look at my favourite hymn and see if we can disappoint the author of the book that I am reading, I am sure we will. The hymn is in the Spiritualists' National Union Hymn Book (Number 89) by T. Moore.

The first Verse says:

Thou art, O God, the life and light
Of all this wondrous world we see;
It's glow by day, its smile by night
Are but reflections, caught from Thee,
Where'er we turn Thy glories shine,
And all things fair and bright are Thine.

This verse tells me that I am living in the light of God,

What a wonderful revelation to know that God's light is an external part of me, that I am never in darkness. Always I am at one with the light that never diminishes, as I live, work and walk with God.

The Author tells us that God is the life and light of all this world, its glow by day provided by the sun, its smile by night provided by the light of the moon and stars, and wherever we look, night or day, we see the reflection of God.

The second verse:

When day, with farewell beams, delays
Among the opening clouds of even,
And we can almost think we gaze
Through golden vistas into heaven,
Those hues that make the sun's decline
So soft, so radiant, Lord are Thine.

In the second verse, the author goes on to say that, as night falls and covers the clouds, the suns rays allow us to gaze at the golden glow which lights up the heavens, so soft, so radiant as the sun dies.

My thoughts tell me that, as day bids us farewell, the night is sent to greet us. We know, without a shadow of a doubt, that a new day will follow. As our thoughts drift into slumber, we soar to heavenly heights, transcending above the clouds into the light and joy of God's presence.

Verse three:

When night, with wings of starry gloom
O'ershadows all the earth and skies,
Like some dark beauteous bird, whose plume
Is sparkling with unnumbered dyes.
That sacred gloom, those fires divine,
So grand, so countless, Lord, are Thine.

This verse reminds me that all of us at times have challenges that may seem difficult to meet or understand. Remember that God is our strength in those dark hours and - centred in God's love - our way is safe and bright and each day can be another step in our growth and spiritual enfoldment. Otherwise, imagine a large bird covering the sky, its body covered with coloured lights, impossible to count.

The fourth verse:

When youthful Spring around us breathes,
Thy spirit warms her fragrant sigh;
And every flower the Summer wreathes
Is born beneath Thy kindling eye;
Where'er we turn Thy glories shine,
And all things fair and bright are Thine.

This hymn tells us that after the winter, the springtime brings new life and everywhere we look is new and fresh; nature is bringing new life in birds and animals, all under the watchful eye of our Father God.

In the springtime of each year, all nature sings a song of beginning again; everywhere we look there is new growth taking place, new life springing forth. Flowers are forming, bright colours are beginning to show, Violets in all their loveliness and Dandelions return in all their persistence.

Sometimes in our personal lives, we need a beginning again time, so let us be receptive to change. We want to see, feel and experience.

Let us bless every sign of new growth, new life in our inner world of thoughts, feelings and emotions. We can trust the blossoming of God's potential in us and thank him for the power to begin again.

Psalm 74 sums up by saying:

The day is thrine, the night is also thrine:
Thou hast prepared the light and the sun

Thou hast set all the borders of the earth:
Thou hast made summer and winter.

Looking at the life story of the author Thomas Moore I discovered that he was born in Dublin Ireland on the 28th of May 1779-1852 a Gemini something I can share as I to was born on the 28th of May, 1931 we must have been drawn together via the spirit friends.

REASSURANCE

At some time in your life you may have had a need to be, reassured.

We all welcome words of encouragement to help us in our daily life. You may find that encouragement and reassurance could be given to you by a friend and if so then you are very fortunate to have someone who is willing to give you their time and those wonderful words of comfort. I'm sure at this time when it is a problem for our young people to find work and the middle-aged are told that they will have to work longer before they can retire, that this world is a very stressful place to be.

The human motive at our work is to please our employer, especially when his eye is upon us, or the monthly turnover figures, but we also need to find satisfaction for ourselves in our work. If you are on the edge of despair, don't give up, hold on to these two words - Perseverance and Courage. You may not be able to feel them, but with your spirit loved ones to help you and guide your steps in the right direction, day by day, will make life's journey easier.

Taking one step at a time helps to slow the journey down. Taking small steps gives us more time to look at our problems, gives us time to take our problems to God in prayer.

We've all had the frustrating experience of trying to contact a major company, only to speak to a disembodied voice that seems intent on ensuring we don't get through to a living human being who can sort our problem out, and after several minutes being told to press this, or enter that, I'm sure, like me, you have put the phone down totally dissatisfied. How we long for someone to listen to us.

Usually, my wife, who is observing my actions, comes to my rescue. She is someone who has all the endurance and patience. I'm sure God has given her staying power to deal with problems calmly, and then the mountain-sized problem shrinks to its true dimension and gets followed by reassurance that everything comes to those who wait and that nothing is perfect.

"Patience is a virtue" was a favourite saying of my mother's, but sadly it does not seem to have been passed on to me, but then I realise she was from the countryside, born on a farm where everything went on so slowly. In her day there were horses that did most of the work, so slowly was the pace. Today's people do not seem to have time to, as the poem says, "stand and stare". Life in the countryside is always interesting. You don't expect exciting things to happen every day, but now and then nature springs a surprise - a black lamb is born, a baby rabbit is found in the flower bed, a pheasant is found feeding with the hens, a duck with its family of chicks, out on a morning exercise. The pattern of family life is much the same as in nature; all are in need of some kind of reassurance. So, if you are in for a tough time today, making a fight for life, or have a health problem, I pray that God will grant you strength, and patience, to see you through the day. And if today your life is a little easier, spare a thought for someone who is having a bad day.

Being patient and taking a long term view of your life will help you achieve your goal. Isn't this the vital point of religion? It shows you things about life, not just today's life, but to look forward into the future and into a life beyond death. This is where we may need some reassurance.

Most religions of the world are full of stories about the Afterlife and how you must live to be able to gain entrance, but, as Spiritualists, you are extraordinary people who should have the knowledge through communication with the Spirit that this Earthly life you are now living continues into the realms of the Spirit World. They blend together into one another; there are no boundaries.

You are the children of the Great Spirit, whose wisdom and love has fashioned the whole universe around you. The whole atmosphere is filled with life. Your own loved ones are there so tune into the spirit life around you and feel their vibrations. Blend yourself to the power that is around and about you, harmonise with the minds of the larger life where you can learn to become a better channel for the inspiration, wisdom, knowledge and truth that is awaiting you, and with your co-operation, hope to be able to spread the message and give reassurance that there is no death.

So many people require this knowledge, which is, to you, commonplace because you have dwelt with it for so long that its acceptance is second nature. This is the greatest pleasure to which we can all look forward to.

RELIGION

If and when religion is mentioned, most people immediately think of the two mainstream religions. We are so sure, indeed, that it may appear entirely unnecessary to ask the question: What is religion?

Nevertheless, I do, for it is remarkable how vague many people are when it comes to a description of what you mean by religion.

A professor Leuba, who is well known in the study of religion, collected forty-nine different definitions of religion and added his own, to make fifty in all. This proved to him that people are uncertain about the subject we know so well. So, what is religion? Shall we be content and say religion is a belief in God? If that is so then we would all have the same religion.

We, as Spiritualists, could say that religion is a belief in spiritual beings. Whilst we maybe content with it, there are those who protest that religion is not what we believe, it's what we do that is important. Some claim religion is more a matter of behaviour than of belief. Is religion a matter of feeling or is it to be in tune with the infinite? Is it to be aware of God directly, as only in such an experience do we clearly see religion manifested at its highest? Why do we trouble about religion at all?

Does Religion really mean anything or nothing to us? This is what we must ask ourselves. There is no halfway position; we either believe or disbelieve, accept it or reject it. If we reject it then truly religion is nothing more than superstition and we pursue it only as a kind of insurance just in case there may be something in it after all.

I am sure you will agree that not many people can say they don't fear death and there are many more who pin their hopes that there is life after this life and surely that in itself is comforting.

There is a power on Earth that is far greater than any material power. The power of the Spirit, without which we can never succeed in utterly transforming not only our lives here on

108

Earth but also the whole of society. This power does not belong to any one person, for the power of Spirit we call "God" is for all who want to live a life that is all important in the positive and creative side that is associated with the present and the future, rather than the past. Religion is about ourselves as individuals. We, as individuals, must try to follow some basic teachings and the simplest ones of all are that we observe the laws of right and wrong and good and bad.

The basic teaching of all religions is of the brotherhood of all people.

Now, we all realise how hard the task is to live a good life, and at no time has the challenge to our personal faith been more insistent than it is today. The world is reeling under brutal aggression towards religion. Many governments would have none and even the two mainstream religious heads would like to dictate to people as to which religion they should follow, hence the politics of religion. The thing we have to observe is that we shall get nowhere if we all take a selfish view. It is, however, teamwork that makes our efforts effective; the less we think of self and the more we concentrate on the general good of our country and the world, the better we shall feel.

For is it not only a moral and a religious precept that selfishness is evil, it is indeed a very practical rule in the working of a democracy. We must all be allowed to have convictions, beliefs, or faith in some sort of moral law, in some kind of right for which we must be prepared to stand up for at all costs. No one should follow any religion without an understanding of that religion. Far too many join our churches without a basic knowledge of Spiritualism. People join our church solely to become clairvoyants, without a thought of the religion.

Religion, especially Spiritualism, is the highest expression of man's power and appeals to the whole man and not simply to half of his nature, yet most religions believe in the immortality of the soul or spirit. For one thing, without such a concept, life is without meaning, purpose, goal, or significance and death is more certain than life. In fact, it is the only event in our personal future of which we can be assured. So what is religion? Is it a way of life? Or is it a way of escape? Some may accept religion is a way of escape; we may try to escape by shutting our eyes to what is before us, or by turning our backs upon what is unpleasant. You will have heard it said: "I would like to get away from it all" but you know you can't, you know you cannot run away from yourself, you have always to come back and face life. We cannot escape the demands of life by running away.

Man has ever sought to use his environment for his own ends, and now we have to ask ourselves to what purpose do we use religion and church for. From experience, I can say this: If anyone abuses either, they will benefit nothing, for Spirit will observe as to the progression of each and all. They will put forward the help needed in your life, but if you, in any way, make a mockery out of your church or your religion, you are on a disaster course.

Let's get one thing straight, religion does not mean that you can bring God into your life and then do what you want. If you bring God into your life then there must have been a need for it in the beginning. So, now we must ask ourselves: Have our lives improved? Have our lives changed for the better? Or have you found a new way to use your church and religion for self?

If you want to go your own way regardless of the rules then go on, live so, but don't expect to be happy. If you want merely animal satisfaction, money, power and don't care how you get them, you may well obtain them all and if you let lust and desire rule your life, surely you cannot expect to be happy. If you ignore the rules, please don't complain at the heartache and misery that inevitable comes to you. The only way to find happiness is to learn this wonderful game of life. This is probably like preaching and we are told that it is easy to preach, or so it appears to those who are not called to do so. If we invent a game then we make the rules, and decide exactly what the players may or may not do to win or even stay in the game at all. Now, this game of life is of God's devising. He makes the rules and you have no right to change them and you certainly have no right to complain. Therefore, should we not try and discover the rules God has invented for this game of life?

We cannot live a life divided because it's impossible to live in God's world on your own terms and be happy. Yes, it's easy to stand aside with calculating eyes shrewdly picking out the weak spots in religion - and you can find them quite easily. It's much easier to discuss religion than to live it. It's easier to criticise the church, its members, its officers and its ministers than it to live a good life. Yes, it's much easier but far less satisfying, which tells us that religion is a personal relationship between the individual and God.

These are my thoughts on the question of what is religion. You will have your own definition.

REUNION

On the 11th of November 1918 was Armistice Day. We, as Spiritualists, call it "Reunion Day", a day when we reunite our thoughts with loved ones who lost their lives in the war. The last large reunion service that I can remember was organised by the then Yorkshire District Council and was held in the town hall in Leeds some thirty years ago, taken by a Miss Doris Johnson of Leeds.

So, on the 11th day of November 1918, after four and a half years of fighting, the guns at last fell silent on the battlefields of Europe, Germany admitted defeat and an armistice was signed.

Since then there has been the Second World War and also war in the far east, the Falklands, Iraq and Afghanistan, all remembered on this day.

Whenever there is a service in our churches, there is always a period of silence and the members of the congregation are invited to think of their friends and loved ones and in silent prayer send them thoughts of healing. I am sure that you have heard it said that "silence is golden", well it certainly is if you have had a noisy day or been irritated by someone else and their taste of music.

To experience silence can be a very precious gift, but sadly our noisy world seems not to appreciate it, however there are times when silence is awkward and we don't know what to say or how to react.

For many, the two minute silence today is a very important feature of our nation's life. It has become a feature of paying respect for some of our nation's tragedies, as well as those further back in the life of our nation.

I read recently in the newspaper of an interview with a young firefighter who attended the scene of the London tube bombing. He spoke movingly of the moment when it became obvious that they were responding to a bomb blast rather than a tube accident as they first imagined. He spoke of the eerie silence that pervaded the carriages of the train. His description was that "It was deafening."

My thoughts go back to the First World War; many old soldiers recalled with wonder the silence that fell over the Flanders battlefield on that far off Christmas day. The magic of Christmas silenced the guns, someone's helmet became a football and then the two sides joined together and raised their voices in song to the carol 'Silent Night', known by all. Photographs were passed around. Then the spell was broken and the horrors of war began again.

Why? That question has been asked over and over again. Will people ever learn to live together in peace and harmony? You and I carry that responsibility, the 'Personal Responsibility', which is the 5th Principle of Spiritualism.

In all walks of life, situations occur in which we have a choice to behave with consideration for others or to turn away, thinking of ourselves.

In this day and age, the pace of life is much faster. The pressure on young people to succeed through study to obtain qualifications causes stress which has to find relief. Some fall to the temptation of alcohol or drugs and many times end up on the wrong side of the law.

Everyone responds to silence differently. Yesterday, I was in Castleford and I sat on a chair in a ladies' fashion shop while my wife looked round. An old lady pushing a shopping basket stopped and spoke to me. She began by saying: "My husband, God bless him, would never come in a shop with me." She said that he had just passed into Spirit but that in the silence of her home she could feel and sense him all around. I felt privileged that Spirit brought her to me.

It is said: "love your enemy". Loving your enemy means acting towards him in the spirit of goodwill, but whilst you may say that is an impossibility when we keep fighting him and dropping bombs and destroying his cities, if we want peace, we will have to practise the spirit of goodwill and it will change to love. To show goodwill towards our enemy means a readiness to believe that the enemy is not expressing his real self in the foul deeds that he does, for there is a lot of bad stuff in the best of us, and certainly there is a lot of good stuff in the worst of us.

113

As a chaplin, I talk to people who are imprisoned. One told me that he never felt alone, he had always someone to talk to and it was possible to find and feel the presence of God in the silence.

So, when you remember this month, what will your experience be? Will the two minute silence be heartfelt or will it be filled with grief for those who lost their lives fighting for us and our country?

At this moment, hymn 345 in the SNU Hymn Book comes to mind:

> *Silently the shades of evening,*
> *Gather round my lonely door;*
> *Silently they bring before me*
> *Faces I have seen before.*
>
> *O, not lost but gone before us!*
> *Let them never be forgot!*
> *sweet their memory to the lonely,*
> *In our hearts they perish not.*
>
> *How such holy memories cluster,*
> *Like the stars when storms have passed;*
> *Pointing up to that fair haven*
> *Where we all shall meet at last.*

This hymn tells us that as the shades of life are drawing to a close on this life, that the love we have for someone cannot be broken by death.

Right now, someone somewhere will be sitting in solitude, so alone in this world and just maybe, in the silence of solitude, their best thoughts may arise. Most of us will never know the blessing that silence can bring and blindly pursue a path through life without tasting the joy of true silence, for it is said that "silence is golden".

SEARCHING FOR THE TRUTH

Movies and TV often show heroes having incredible adventures - exploring in space, rediscovering lost cities, finding a way out of some impossible situation, or saving the world from destruction.

The actors, who play these parts, have us spellbound and bring a real excitement into our lives. This is how you should feel when you enter your church, for there you will find that that is where excitement unfolds and is more tangible and far more exciting and interesting than any film plot. You are in a place where you can receive directions that will elevate you. We do not demand that you believe without question, we are seekers of the truth. Use your own observation and understanding and listen carefully to the philosophy given from the platform, some better than others. Evaluate with an open mind, observe and investigate, decide if this way of life is right for you. Reach your own conclusion.

Remember, evaluated experiences lift you above the crowd. People who make it a practice to reflect on their experiences and learn from them are rare. The truth is that experience is costly; you cannot gain experience without paying a price and hopefully you will get value for the price that you pay and at the end of life, you should know that you will have to pay for the failures that you have encountered.

We believe that death is merely the disintegration of the physical body and that there is an Afterlife to the spirit, or soul, which continues living. Those who have strong bonds with relatives or friends left on Earth will sometimes communicate with them through mediums. Spiritualists are continually explaining to non-Spiritualists that "we cannot and do not contact those who have passed on, it is those in the Spirit World who return." You cannot command help from the Spirit World, all you can do is to put yourself in the right condition to receive it. When you are spiritually ready, the higher power will reach you. Never forget that you are essential to the scheme; you were born with all the equipment needed mentally, physically and spiritually. It is up to you to use it, provided by God as part of your divine heritage.

The purpose of this life is that the good within should control and dominate your life. The things of the Spirit are found in the warm, simple way of life. In love and human kindness and in this way, we can create a brotherhood of all people, and as we become more sensitive and aware of the Spirit around us, we will notice, by our thoughts, speech and actions, that we have progressed. If we pursue this way of life, we will find the true meaning of love and then endeavour to lead and inspire by example, which is to search for and encourage good ideas coming from the World of Spirit.

I was told at a young age that "patience is a virtue." There are great benefits to waiting, for example; if you learn to wait and observe, you will make better choices. I like to see my garden neat and tidy, but I'm slow at getting the inspiration to change to perspiration. My great ideas don't become reality because I don't spend the time and energy to make them happen. I realise that if I don't cultivate life's garden, it also will suffer and not look at its best. Everything we grow, be it material or spiritual, needs our best efforts if we want the best fruits of our labours, but with perseverance and regular practice, this spiritual inspiration will gradually give rise to an abiding inward tranquillity which will impart strength and love to the soul wherever it goes. The peace of the garden will unfold and the emotions, purified and blessed by the Spirit, will flow out and enfold those in need of sympathy and healing.

We must not be ignorant of our true being; the Earthly body is not permanent, for it passes away at the end of this mortal life. Whilst we live on Earth, most people never give it a thought and may never know of the more important body which remains unseen to the human eye, though ever present around us all.

Being spiritual and of finer substance than material things and while it is not seen by normal vision, it is never the less assured. This is our 'real' body for therein dwells the life and the true personality with all its attributes and at death is disassociated from human form to enter a life more real and without end.

116

The so-called 'death', dreaded by many, is but the natural escape of the living spirit from the bonds of its Earthly covering and will evolve to a world of greater activity.

All of us are Spirit, with everlasting life, for such is in accordance with the divine plan and no one can evade it. Those who prove faithful here will have a place of responsibility in the World of Spirit. Knowing this ought to give us a true purpose to our lives in this world. Our eternal honour and employment will depend upon the way we have conducted ourselves in this life.

Life is a continuous and expanding process. The purpose of this life is to build a character that is fitting for the next part of your life's journey. These are the school days of the spirit; learn your lessons well so that you can move into the greater existence beyond. You can always rise higher because you will be in a world of eternal progress. Spiritualism is a science, a philosophy and a religion; a way of life, all in one. It is the growth of the spirit into the whole being. Your life is an expanding process, be aware of the beauty and goodness in God's world, for many times the heavenly messengers come, bringing us heavenly blessings, but we are so intent on Earthly things that we do not see them or open the door.

If we would but train ourselves to be more aware of those spirit friends who accompany us through life then when they knock on the door we will be ready to give a loving welcome. The parallel to life on Earth is profound; it really does not make any difference how the world ranks your status because the fact of your birth gives you a divine heritage. All noble life must be inspired by the Spirit; we must seek the brightest and the best to work with. A good motto for life is to live for immortal things.

SPIRITUALISM

Spiritualism is not, as is commonly believed, a sinister cult, meeting in darkened rooms to call up the dead, it is a recognised religious movement, with its own churches and ministers, who possess the same rights and privileges as other religions.

Spiritualism is, in itself a religion in that it embodies the main idea of all religions - that there is life after death, immortality and the existence of a god. Spiritualists are often accused of being atheists or anti-Christian but I say here and now that Spiritualists are not anti-Christian, any more than they are anti-Jewish, anti-Hindu, or anti-Muslim. Spiritualism is a universal religion, recognising such leaders as Buddha, Muhammad and Moses, as well as Jesus.

One difference between Spiritualism and the orthodox Christian religion is embodied in our 'Principles', of which there are seven. The Fifth Principle is "Personal Responsibility", so we do not accept the fact that Jesus died on the cross to save us from our sins. We hold that no one can do this but ourselves; we are given free will and the ability to distinguish between right and wrong and we alone are responsible for all our thoughts and actions.

Further, we do not believe in a vindictive God sitting in judgment over us. We are our own judge, here and now and we receive compensation or retribution for whatever we have done good or bad. Heaven and hell are not places to which we are destined to go but states of mind of our own creation. We do not automatically become spiritual when we leave this world, we shall infact retain our Earthly characteristics while the opportunity will be given throughout eternity to make spiritual progress and so undo any wrongs we have committed on Earth, for free will and personal responsibility will still be with us in the world to come. Another difference is that we cannot accept that children are born in sin; therefore, we do not have christenings, we have a naming service using flowers, which are used as a symbol of purity and grace.

We are now living in a material age where religion has lost its impact; therefore, science tells us that any religion that can overcome this materialist influence must be scientific. Spititualism is just that, it has turned the pious hope of a hereafter into a scientific fact. The advent of the spirit of man into this world - and in the course of time his transition to another world - is a scientific fact proven by mediumship. Spiritualism bows to no creeds or dogmas; its philosophy is centred around seven principles, which came into being through the mediumship of Emma Hardinge Britten and so established the following unalterable seven principles of Spiritualism as the basis of the religion and religious philosophy of the Spiritualists' National Union. These Principles were also required to be used to define Spiritualism and Spiritualists when the government recognised it as a religion.

It should be born in mind that these principles are not commandments and in accepting them, one is accorded complete liberty of interpretation. The Seven Principles are as follows:

1. The Fatherhood of God

The First Principle allows each of us to have his or her own idea of God. To some, he is an austere personality, seated on a throne in heaven, instilling fear in his believers and meting out wrathful judgment to wrongdoers. To others, he is a benign father, caring for his vast family of every creed and colour and personified in everything around us that is beautiful. The latter is the broad viewpoint as envisaging the one supreme power.

So we regard God as a supreme power; the author of a divine plan. The natural law through which the universe he created is governed based on love, not fear and is the controlling force of all. The greatest central source of all life and love.

When we transgress these laws, we are betraying a trust for which we shall have to pay here or in the life hereafter. Our relationship with God is, therefore, determined by our obedience to these laws.

2. The Brotherhood of Man

If we accept The Fatherhood of God then it naturally follows that we are his children - brothers and sisters in one family of all races and colours and this confers upon us a dual responsibility to God the Father and to each other, which we can sum up in one word - service. The equalities of modern society, of rich and poor, weak and strong, wise and ignorant, provide for an intensive love and service in our daily lives.

We all have something to give. We meet those who need material help and we can give encouragement, a kind word, or just a smile. One small act may work wonders, and if we would extend this call of service beyond the confines of our family, our town and country and out into the outside world, pain and suffering, turmoil and wars, would cease and we would bring into being that peace which passes all understanding.

It goes further than that. The real meaning of our existence is our obligation to our fellow man, he is also a spirit here on Earth and immortal. The Brotherhood of Man is extended into the spirit spheres.

The Second Principle - The Brotherhood of Man tells us the existence and identity of the individual continues after the change we call 'death'.

3. Communion of Spirits and the Ministry of Angels

This is the key around which our whole philosophy turns. For more than 150 years, Spiritualism has proved conclusively that man not only survives death, but is able, through mediums, to commune with those left behind.

The people who we call "mediums" are so highly sensitive to the spirit vibrations that they are able to establish contact with those who have passed over and wish to contact us.

We all have spirit guides, or helpers (a guardian angel, if you like), who use the medium as an instrument through whom they can talk. We are thus able to learn how our loved ones are faring in their new way of life; this proof of survival is of great help to those who are bereaved. The Communion of Spirits and the Ministry of Angels says that, under suitable conditions, communications take place between us here on Earth and the inhabitants of the Spirit World into which we all pass.

4. Continuous Existence of the Human Soul

All greater religions of the world subscribe to some form of life after death in some nebulous, heavenly existence - but they have failed to prove it. Spiritualism, on the other hand, does prove this fact in no uncertain manner, and in doing so has profoundly revolutionised our lives in that our behaviour is not encompassed within the narrow limits of our Earthly lives but extends to eternity. Our mode of living here will determine our spiritual status in the life to come.

This principle tells us that each individual reaps that what they have sown, with favour to none and takes their happiness or unhappiness into their new surroundings.

5. Personal Responsibility

This principle is the major difference between Spiritualism and other religions. The basis of the Christian religions rests on a belief that Jesus died on the cross to save us from our sins. This, we strongly repudiate. Jesus lived in political times and was put to death for political reasons. As I said at the beginning, Spiritualism asserts that no one can save us from wrongdoings but ourselves.

Man, through his conscience, knows the difference between right and wrong and is given free will to choose which path to take. No one, be they religious or atheist, can escape the consequences of their own mistakes. What others call "sin", we regard as a violation of the divine law made by God. Personal Responsibility tells us that each individual is their own saviour and cannot look to someone else to bear his/her sins and suffer for his/her mistakes

6. Compensation and Retribution hereafter for all the good and evil deeds done on Earth

Past teachings tell us that, at the end of this life, we would come before our maker, sitting on a throne of judgement; this would be our judgment day here and it would be decided whether we would be allowed into God's heavenly kingdom or cast into the fiery furnaces in hell. Now, heaven and hell are states of mind of our own creation and not celestial localities, so our code of conduct on this Earth will determine our spiritual status in the World of Spirit.

It is equally wrong to think that because one attends church regularly, or performs evangelical or other good work, that one will automatically be given pride of place in the hereafter. It will be our everyday deeds and motives that will count.

We know that our conduct must be guided by the Golden Rule, first proclaimed by Confucius, of doing to others as we would wish to be done to ourselves.

7. Eternal Progresses open to every human Soul

The idea of eternal progress may seem hard to understand in this world where everything has an ending, but in the world to come (call it what you will), where there are no clocks or calendars, time is immaterial. Spiritualism points to the certainty of eternal progress, but the rate of our own particular advancement will depend on one's desire to do so, remembering we still have free will.

We shall be by no means idle in the World of Spirit; in fact, we shall be extremely busy perusing those paths which lead us towards perfection. And we shall have eternity in which to do it.

The transition from our Earthly life does not alter our present make-up or character; we shall be just the same as we were before our passing, retaining our free will to fashion our new life with the sure knowledge that we shall be given the opportunity to make spiritual progress. With no limit to time or the height that we can reach. Once again, we come face-to-face with our personal responsibilities even on the other side.

The Seven Principles dispel despair and give a feeling of hope and satisfaction, so everyone should do his or her best to diffuse kindness, love, sympathy, justice and tolerance. They all make for increased Happiness.

STARTING YOUR SEARCH

It has long been felt that a need exists for some form of guidance for our public workers, the church officers and exponents who present Spiritualism to the public at large.

The increasing interest in Spiritualism spurs us on to raise our standards and to be ready for the challenge. All workers, mediums, speakers, chairpersons, church officers etc. must be able to speak clearly and get their message across, whether from the higher realm, or from our humble selves. The ability to clearly project oneself must be required as the first step in the personal development which is associated with the expansion of the gifts and the work, which we are pursuing.

We are concerned with presentation - the manner in which our behaviour is used to represent the inner self, the ability to convey to others the vitality of one's personal involvement with the subject under discussion, together with clear simple integrity of purpose.

We do not want to become theatrical, but we can learn from the actor and the salesman, for our task is, in a way, to sell ourselves and our religion, not for us to make a profit and become grand. We want people who are listening to us to reap the benefits and feel relaxed in our presence.

Presentation is the method of properly communicating an awareness of ourselves as personalities. People who have taken the platform too soon cannot offer a good standard of work to the defenceless public. Let us then consider what we wish to find in our ideal exponent: Quite apart from any mediumistic abilities which lie outside our present term of reference, self-confidence and self-control together form part of the essential tools to the public worker. Self-confidence is a state of mind and can be cultivated. As we live our lives, we become creatures of habit.

"Habit" means to repeat an action until it becomes second nature; a mental condition acquired by practice. If we can accept this definition then we are all perfectly able to cultivate the habit of self-control by practice. If we make a habit to smile warmly and feel the warmth within us radiating out then we will accordingly give and receive of that same warmth. We might quite wrongly cultivate the habit of frowning with appropriate result. If we habitually adopt a free and easy stance, and at the same time offer a friendly outgiving of ourselves to people, then we will usually be received in the same way and the cycle of reproducing will build on this happy note.

We must bear in mind that self-confidence depends, to a greater extent, on knowledge, knowledge of oneself and knowledge of the subject.

The chairperson is very important, he or she sets the scene. I think that being prepared and confident, having a list of announcements ready to hand, not pausing and having to search around for their lists, introducing the speaker with words well thought out to inspire the speaker, and kindle the interest of the congregation, is vital. The chairperson represents the church and people judge the church from their first impressions. Looking good is important and that goes for dress too, neat and tidy. We Spiritualists are proud of our religion. We command respect so, yes, the chairperson has the first message.

So, we come to the medium. How long does it take to become a good medium? Certainly, hours given to development, years to progress efficiently, and lucky are those who began in the lyceum. That is where we should be most concerned, with the teaching of the young. To come back to development, some people have developed a psychic faculty in a narrow field, decided "this is it" and often, regrettably, have an overdeveloped sense of self-importance and go no further, missing out on greater achievements and losing out themselves spiritually.

The student must realise that development goes on. Even the best mediums need to continue improving by regular meditation, all striving to give of their very best, for inspiration will be given to those who earnestly seek spiritual growth. Maurice Barbanell wrote: "When you learn to live in harmony with this power, you will derive from life the richness, lustre and nobility which are your rightful heritage and you will fulfil your divine destiny."

An old saying tells us: "Fail to prepare, prepare to fail."

Best wishes in your search.

STILL LOOKING BACK

Some time ago, I wrote about being in the right place at the right time; a time and place where you are needed in one way or another. Sometimes it may be for your own benefit or in some way where you can give help to others. As a Spiritualist, you should be more aware than others of these happenings.

Just before Christmas, I went to the butchers; this takes me past the churchyard. As I walked past the gate, I noticed a young lady standing by a grave. Obviously, she had lost a loved one. My thoughts said: Tell her that there are no dead, but then I thought that she might not be able to accept my view, so I stood still, thinking: "If she comes my way, I will express a word of sympathy", but it was not to be, for she got in a car and left .

As I arrived at the butchers, it had started to rain heavily. Still a little disappointed, the shop was full. I was outside the door and an old lady opened it, saying to the other people: "Move up, this man's getting wet." Upon entering, I said to her: "It isn't fit to bring a dog out." Her reply was: "I have a walk every day, it helps to keep me active and it's nice to get out of the house, but going home to an empty house is not very pleasant." She told me that her husband had died three years ago and that he had a lovely passing. He just came home from his daily walk, sat in his favourite chair and said: "It's time to go" and he passed away. Then she said to my surprise: "He's not dead, you know, for he comes many times and sits in his chair as large as life and we talk and when I've had enough of him, I tell him: 'Go home cheeky' (that was her pet name for him). My family think I am mad." I said: "I do not think you are, because I know it can happen."

Can you imagine the scene? Everybody went silent, the butcher and the entire queue were looking towards us. She looked at them and emphasising said: "I know this, that there is no death." So here I was, in the right place at the right time, listening to someone telling me that there is no death, someone who may never have been to a Spiritualist church and had probably never heard of Spiritualism and yet may have seen and experienced more than most. My turn came and I realised all eyes were still focused in our direction. What an experience! I got served and as I left, she took my hand and wished me a very happy Christmas.

I arrived home and told my wife about my encounter. It was then that I realised how privileged I was and that every minute of time is precious.

If we go around not having time for others, we will miss so much. It's up to us as to what kind of a day we have and what kind of contribution we can make in the short time we have each day. Every night we should look back at our day and ask ourselves: Have we done our best? For there are many ways we can help and cheer those less fortunate than ourselves. God uses those less fortunate than we are to put us to the test. You will find that a few moments given to others will open a window and you will see something for which to be thankful.

If there is something that calls for action, tackle it but if the issue is obscure and you are not sure, stand still and give the problem time to settle itself. Words are so easily spoken and we forget what power they have; they can bring pleasure or pain; they seem to vanish so quickly the moment that they have dropped from our lips.

We forget that they do not go away, but linger like arrows in the heart, or like the fragrant flowers. When we talk with others, we should try to speak some thoughtful words before we part. Words that will give help, strength and hope to cheer them on their way, as we may never meet again.

SURVIVAL OF THE SPIRIT

Whilst working with members of other religions, I have become interested as to what they believe regarding life after death, so I have searched books and asked questions and realise that. from the beginning of civilisation, there has been a widespread belief in the survival of the spirit after death in a place where it lives on.

Ideas of what happens after death and of the Afterlife vary greatly; different religions and cultures have their own beliefs. The ancient Greeks thought that the spirit after death was thought to be of a highly attenuated or shadowy nature, existing in some dim underworld called Hades. In other cases, there was a definite idea that the Spirit World was very similar to the material world, that it was a continuation of it on a higher plane and that the spirit had a real and substantial existence as in Earth life.

With the advancement of civilisation and the recognition of certain moral values, there arose the belief that those who led a good life on Earth, by observing an accepted moral standard of religious rites, were allowed to enter an ideal state of existence, but those who had lead an evil life were punished for their misdeeds by being forced to go into a place of endless torment (hell) from which there was no escape.

At first, it was generally held by the Jews that there was no resurrection of the dead and that a person survived merely in the lives and minds of his or her children and descendants, but later they arose as a shadowy kind of existence in an underworld.

According to the teachings of the ancient Greeks, the spirit at death passed to an underworld, or Hades, where it was either rewarded for its good deeds or punished for its evil ones. In the former case, it was reborn as a human being, and in the latter as an animal. This transmigration of the spirit, which had passed through three good lives and had been found guiltless three times, was allowed to enter Elysium, the land of the blessed.

So, the ancient Greeks believed in the transmigration of the soul, as did the Egyptians and as do the druids and it is still an important doctrine in Hinduism and Buddhism, two of the most important religions in the world.

The druids believe that if a man has led a brave and victorious life, his spirit goes at once to Flath Innis or Elysian Island, or Heaven; however, if he had led a bad life, his spirit returned to Earth as an animal and then at death he was reincarnated again as a man. This procedure was repeated until his spirit was fit to go to Elysian Island.

In early Druid teaching, an evil person was not reincarnated but went to Infurin, the isle of the cold land and fierce animals. According to the Hindu and Buddhist religions, man passes through a series of Earth lives in which he ascends or descends on the spiritual scale depending whether those lives are good or evil. This progression of the spirit, up or down, obeys what is termed "The law of the deed of Karma", which states that from good must come good and from evil must come evil. By leading a succession of good lives, a man ultimately reaches the ideal state of bliss (Nirvana) in Buddhism, but a series of evil causes him to fall lower and lower spiritually until he may reincarnate as an animal or insect, or as a plant.

With different religions there has been a greater variation in beliefs of what constitutes the ideal after death state, or heaven. To some, it is a place of light and rest, to others it is a land where they would be united with their saviour or god.

The Egyptians believed that the spirit, after death, had a cycle of disembodied existence for thousands of years and then returned again to inhabit the original physical body; hence, the necessity for preserving by mummification.

Other descriptions of heaven are Elysium, or Meadow, on which grew a perfusion of eternal flowers. Homer described Elysium as "a beautiful meadow at the western extremity of the earth, on the banks of the river Oceanus" where the spirit led a life of perfect happiness, no snow, nor rain, nor storm, but the cool west wind breathe there forever.

The Native American Indian of North America conceived heaven as the "happy hunting ground", a land of lakes and forests with cool streams and an ideal climate. So, it is evident that people imagined their heaven largely by the conditions under which they had lived on Earth. For example, those who suffered hardship imagined a life of plenty, those who were imprisoned. in many ways see heaven as place of freedom, likewise, those who lived in the hot sandy desert thought of heaven as a fertile, shady, well-watered oasis (a Garden of Eden) in which they dwelt in tents with beautiful women.

In contrast to this The Wandering, or Nomadic Northmen of the cold, far north of Europe, who were often half-starved, living in frozen conditions, conceived the spirit of the dead after a day of sport and could sit at night before a huge fire, feasting and drinking.

Christians believe in a heaven and hell; those who have not lived a good life will go to the fiery furnace to suffer endless agonies from heat and thirst and see heaven as a place of endless worship and adoration of God, a celestial city gleaming with precious stones and beautiful pearly gates and golden streets where all their longings for plenty, human fellowship, comfort and happiness, would be satisfied. Many people prefer not to think about the Afterlife because it calls up repressed fear about death.

Spiritualists see heaven as the Spirit World or Summerland, a place where they must grow spiritually, a place of service where knowledge can be gained and although there are many names for the next world, I think that I still prefer the old fashioned name of "paradise."

Entry into the higher Spirit Realms is not dependent upon any belief in a creed, religious dogma, or baptism. There is no doubt that certain religions provide a better atmosphere, or training ground, for spiritual development in Earth's life than others, and while there is a measure of truth in all religions of the world, not one, by itself has the full truth, nor does it point the only way to God.

I believe that we evolve our characters and personalities while we are here on Earth. We cannot cheat.

On arriving in the next dimension of life, taking with us only our good side, every thought, every deed, arrives with us; however, circumstances of the life we have lived are taken into consideration. Sometimes what we thought was bad is seen in a different light. We judge ourselves harshly.

There will be the opportunity to progress by service to those less fortunate than ourselves, and who knows, we may be on a higher level of progression than we imagined.

This hymn 'Lord, We Thank Thee for the Pleasure' seems to tell us to be gratful for this Earthly life:

Lord, we thank Thee for the pleasure
That our happy lifetime gives,
For the boundless worth and treasure
Of a soul that ever lives;
Mind that looks before and after,
Lifting eyes to things above;
Human tears, and human laughter,
And the depths of human love.

For the thrill, the leap, the gladness
Of our pulses flowing free;
E'en for every touch of sadness
That may bring us nearer Thee;
But, above all other kindness,
Thine unutterable love,
Which, to heal our sin and blindness,
Sent Thy dear Son from above.

Teach us so our days to number
That we may be early wise;
Dreamy mist, or cloud, or slumber,
Never dull our heav'nward eyes.
Hearty be our work and willing,
As to Thee, and not to men;
For we know our soul's fulfilling
Is in Heav'n, and not 'til then.

Words: Thomas Jez-Blake, 1855
Music: Cyril Taylor, 1941.
© ABBOT'S LEIGH

TEAMWORK

Saturdays have always been a day for sport, and when the season ends, it seems that our life becomes void of something to talk about. Yes, Saturday is a day to knock, throw, or kick a ball.

In life, we have all experienced knocks and we seem to be thrown in every direction and I am sure we feel that we have been kicked around many times.

Now, we all know about teamwork, that if the team is going to succeed then all the players must work together towards the common goal. Every team wants to win the FA Cup; it's the dream of every player to lift the cup from underneath the stadium's iconic arch, but before this, we have to remember that the road to Wembley starts months before the final match. There are always the favourites, the form book suggests this and makes them odds on to win, but you know that sometimes there is an underdog who on the day excels and upsets the odds despite the fact that they are the poorest team, but by working together and having nothing to lose, they show that teamwork wins through. They face the challenge together, turning around what has been a difficult year.

Now, it's not just the players on a sports field who face daunting situations and challenging circumstances. We all face times when life threatens to overwhelm us, when we are uncertain, or when the problems we face seem more than we can cope with. These are the times we can feel weighed down, the future looks bleak, it seem that no one understands or cares, we feel so alone.

The good news is that we do not have to face these problems on our own. No matter how overwhelming the odds are or how daunting the situation, just remember that your Father God will support you. The power of the Spirit will help you through the tough times in your life, so do not ever be afraid to team up with God. He is your best defence.

When I played football, I never heard the phrase "professional foul" but today it is accepted as normal. They say that matches can be won on the drawing board, and footballers today do not seem half as fit and prepared, for the task in hand. I know that in my spiritual life, if there is any foul play, then I am aware that I have broken my vows and that I will have to accept the consequences. As for planning ahead, that's ok if everything goes to plan. Many years ago when I joined the army, my mother wrote on a small card these words: "Man can plan, but God will decide."

During my life, I have seen many changes on the sports field. The rules have been revised, the games have been speeded up, the goalkeeper has to kick the ball more. In rugby league, kicking has been minimised, and where there were heavy forwards, now they are fast and fit, Cricket has also changed. Instead of the three-day matches, which often got bogged down, there is what is called "20-20 cricket." It speeds up the game as there are only a certain amount of overs to be played and the team that gets the most runs wins. This means the players have to throw caution to the wind, they have to take more risks if they want to win. 20-20 cricket may lack some of the old coaching manual shots on how to protect the wicket, but the crowd loves it because there is no room to play safety shots, attack is the best form of defence (he who dares wins), batsmen get one chance and a split second to pick their shot, so sometimes they have to take risks.

Away from the ground, how is your 'innings' going? At most funerals I have attended someone says: "They had a good innings." Sometimes in life we get caught out and find that we are on a sticky wicket. The reality is that we only get one shot at life and only in this life does God offer us a chance of eternal life.

When you take the Spiritualist bat, you are batting to protect your whole self. The risks are slim if you follow your principles; remember at all times that you are batting for a place in that eternal home in God's presence.

We have to ask ourselves: Have the changes in the game improved it, made it more exciting, or even better? Are the rules easier to understand, has it brought more people to watch? Well, it seems all are functioning very well.

Now is the time to pick our team. What position do you desire? Do you want to be a striker, a goalscorer? They seem to be always in the forefront. You could be a defender, a centre-back who controls the defence and a midfielder who takes the ball forward and feeds the forward line; he is the one who has the responsibility to be up with the forwards in attack... and in defence when needed.

Friends, just think, this is your life. In life we do all these things - at work, in family life, or in any organisation in which we serve. Now we have to remember the backroom staff who prepare everything for the big day; without them nothing would be possible. The groundsmen, the cleaners, tea ladies and many more. At the top comes the management and of course, the main directors.

Now, I will ask my manager, my Father God for his help to improve my abilities in every position he asks me to play.

But remember, teamwork is the glue that brings it all together.

THE ANIMAL KINGDOM

Many people in this world see the lives of animals as very cheap. Man looks at the animal kingdom as something to use and abuse. We see animals killed and fed to other animals and we consider them as the weaker form of life, existing only for the nourishment of the people of this world.

We maim and kill. We have created situations in which millions of people starve while others store grain in silos and destroy gallons of milk and other commodities to keep prices high.

We look upon one another as prey, to satisfy our emotional and physical needs; in fact it's a dog eat dog world and to live in it we must take advantage of others before they take advantage of us. We look at life as a contest that produces winners and losers; our behaviour and values are so much shaped by perceptions that lack reverence that we forget what it is like to be humble. The human race has become arrogant; we behave as though this world belongs to us and we can do whatever we want to it; we pollute the land, the oceans and the atmosphere without thinking of the needs of other life forms that live upon the Earth.

Now, we, as Spiritualists, can join with the people who care for this world and about the people who live in it.

Respect is an attitude of honouring life. Man kills and calls it sport, but to be respectful means accepting all life in itself of some value. We Spiritualists must learn to live with reverence, which means we must be willing to say: That is life, we must not harm it. We must ask ourselves: Is this the way to treat the animal kingdom that serves us so patiently? The spiritual person cannot consider him or herself superior to another being.

We are told to love one another and love is a tonic we all can share. When our actions create disorder, we ourselves in this life, or in another, will feel that disorder, but if our actions create harmony, we also come to feel that harmony. This will allow us to experience the effect that we have created.

In the midst of all this, the basic human qualities of live and let live and fair play will have to be expressed. If they are not then our society will turn rancid and decay.

Our primary needs are to be fed, clothed and housed. The rule of law and the freedom of opinion and speech are necessary in any decent ordering of life, but if we desire a good life, a lot more will be required from us all. We could build a new world in which men and women would find fellowship and fullness of life.

The feeling is universal, we must have more respect for life and its fullest expression, for it means an attitude of reverence to all life, including animals and nature, as well as the human race.

Nature has a multitude of variety and charm. This world is a storehouse, it has treasures hidden in the air and the earth with its stores of wonders untold, and in the cruel sea we find all kinds of wonderful things that the Great Creator has lavishly displayed for the interest of us all.

The ways and habits of plants and other forms of life are each found to be especially suited to their environment and clearly show that nothing has been overlooked or found to be ill-fitting; everything fits perfectly in the design of the Great Creator.

Even the grass underfoot is full of delicate grace and beauty, created for the welfare and interest of man and beast. Everywhere I see evidence of what God can do.

Once again, I turn to my SNU Hymn Book, hymn number 186 by Lizzie Doten. She writes where God can be seen and found:

God of the Granite and the rose!
Soul of the sparrow and the bee!
The mighty tide of being flows
Through countless channels, Lord, from Thee.
It leaps to life in grass and flowers,
Through every grade of being runs,
Till, from creation's radiant towers,
Its glory flames in stars and suns.

O ye who sit and gaze on life
With folded hands and fettered will,
Who only see, amid the strife,
The dark supremacy of ill,
Know, that like birds, and streams and flowers,
The life that moves you is divine!
Nor time, nor space, nor human powers,
Your god-like spirit can confine.

God of the granite and the rose!
Soul of the sparrow and the bee!
The mighty tide of being flows
Through all thy creatures back to Thee,
Thus round and round the circle runs,
A mighty sea without a shore,
While men and angels, stars and suns,
Unite to praiseThee evermore.

This hymn, when written by Lizzie Doten, was fifteen verses long, but these three I have heard and sung many times over the years as a Spiritualist.

It shows the quality of her mediumship and provides evidence that life is eternal. It also shows how mediums can use their talents to help people with their grief. Spiritualism removes the barriers of life after death, and through mediums, provides the best kind of knowledge of the Afterlife. They can also bring comfort to those who grieve .

THE BUTTERFLY EFFECT

Wanting a picture of a butterfly, I went on my laptop and found the "Butterfly Effect", which asked: "Would the flap of a butterfly's wings in Brazil alter the direction of a tornado in Texas?" You would not think that the tiny wings of a butterfly could make a difference to the weather conditions in another country many hundreds of miles away.

Just imagine, then, if thoughts are living things and we could, as the butterfly, alter conditions across the world, be it for good or bad. Your loving, healing thought prayers can release the power of God and activate the power of the Spirit to go to work in any situation needed, anywhere across this world.

You may not realise that good and bad thoughts come from the same instrument, for as you send out thoughts of love and care for someone, they will return to you, as all good or bad thoughts do. (You reap what you sow.)

You must foster love and goodness in your thoughts, send a thought for healing and live in an atmosphere of hope and love which will bring serenity around you.

Working with Spirit means that at all times you have to be prepared, for at any given moment you could find yourself in the presence of someone who is in need of help, comfort, or encouragement. The Spirit uses those who have enough compassion and if you are willing to reach out and embrace others and stop long enough to listen, you will begin to realise that God will use you to bring them healing and hope.

And so your life becomes a continual state of preparation. To work for the Spirit, do not idle away the opportunities given to you. The fact that you open your mind to receive more truth means that you make yourself more accessible to those who are capable of supplying your needs. Your spirit workers work extremely hard to extract from you the best results and try not to let you make the mistakes that they may have done.

137

You may not see or hear them and you may not feel their presence, but that is not a reason for you to think that they are not near at hand, for one knows that we canhear the wind blow but we cannot see it; a deaf person cannot hear the birdsong, yet they do sing, and we could again refer to the 'butterfly effect' that someone in another part of the world, or in this case the universe, may be responsible for things that are going on in our daily lives.

Are your experiences full of stops and starts? If so, then you must overcome the fear of failure, and when you fail, try again, for history shows us that failure can be a bridge to success, and remember, you can't create the future by dwelling in the past and who knows, your next move may lead to a new and more rewarding career.

Every so often it's good to ask yourself: Why do I do nothing instead of getting on with my daily tasks, leaving things for tomorrow? People who fail to make the most of opportunities, or fail to follow their responsibilities, hurt only themselves for we know that tomorrow never comes. It might seem as if there's always work to do and no time for rest and pleasure, but remember, you are in control of your agenda for life; now is the time to upgrade and improve yourself and move forward in all your endeavours.

So, when you assign yourself to a task or project, put all your effort in to it, extracting from the project all the satisfaction possible. Your task may be helpful to others but just maybe, when you have completed it, you might find that you have enhanced your own divinity.

We are all small and appear to be the same but as we grow older our true beauty shows; like a butterfly, we are all different, and beautiful in our own way. When a child asks about death, what better way to explain it to them than the reproduction of the butterfly. It lays its eggs on leaves desirable as food and then, when the caterpillar bursts out from the egg, eats enough food until then it is time to find a spot, weave a cocoon and waits until it is time to be reborn into a butterfly.

When we are born and grow, our parents see that we have food, but like all living creatures, at some time in our lives, we have to die, but then after a short sleep, awaken in heaven, clothed like a butterfly. It may not be acceptable by all, but could ease troubled minds.

Our life is a journey and while we are journeying, it is important for us to enjoy the trip; enjoy every moment as you travel through your life. So enjoy this moment and thank God for the gifts placed in your pathway as a new day is born.

The hymn by Thomas Carlyle (1795 -1881) comes to mind:

So here hath been dawning
Another blue day,
Think, wilt thou let it,
Slip useless away.

Out of eternity,
This new day is born;
Into eternity,
At night will return.

Behold it aforetime.
No eye ever did;
So soon it forever,
From all eyes is hid.

Here Hath been dawning,
Another blue day.
Think, wilt thou let it,
Slip useless away?

Each dawn brings light into this world, and at night it dies in darkness, only to be reborn in another blue day.

THE EFFECT OF MUSIC

The effect of music on a person may be sad or happy. It can bring back memories and although the tune could be a happy tune, it could bring back a sad occasion. Music can take you back in time to childhood memories; it can bring an instant change of mood.

Music and colours are inseparable. Each note in the scale has its own colour and music brings colour into our lives. Many songs have been written about colour, e.g. *Red Roses for a Blue Lady, 'When the Blue of the Night Meets the Gold of the Day, There's a Rainbow Round My Shoulders* and *Tie a Yellow Ribbon Around The Old Oak Tree*. We feel that the composer had a reason to put colour into music; as the artist sees and paints a picture, composers see music as a picture. Music and colour cannot be separated.

We know that music can stir people into action, soldiers into battle and marching, and if you have stood on a football ground on match day, you realise that music inspires the crowd to sing its team to victory. Music can be emotional and touch the heart. This tells us that everyone is like a note of music and each person has their own sound and each and everyone has a key note. If we can blend each one together, we get harmony. Older people complain that today's music is too loud and noisy, but to the young people it is music to their ears.

Through spiritual awareness, attitudes can change. Music is love and powerful music is energy and tenderness, all representing God. What we have learned is that we must have tolerance and an understanding of each other. I believe that the Spirit blends together groups of people who are in attunement and on the same note of vibration.

A change comes, as I am reading a book that I truly think was sent to me from the spirit friends via one of my Earthly friends. It begins with a quote from the author, which states that "there is no need to quote examples of hymns through which we can express our thankfulness to God."

140

My opinion here differs from the author. I feel that an understanding of the Spiritualist hymn book can and will prove to you and I that hymns can speak to our emotions, our consciences and our wills. People have been truly inspired by the Spirit to bring and join words of wisdom and music together, just as words and music inspire the congregation, bringing them closer together, as they sing out praises to God.

THE GOOD LIFE

During World War II, I was a young boy, and although we were so young, we were aware of the word "conflict". At that time it was an everyday word, but after the war it was forgotten until Remembrance Day came around. However, over the last two or three years, it has become an everyday word once again. All over the world people are in conflict, but it does not stop there, we have conflict in governments, in Religion, and in everyday life, and yes, in the family. To be good is not enough, to practice and live by any creed is not enough. The infinite is to be experienced, not learnt.

Many people have passed through this world being good but have never known an infinite relationship with the absolute force of Spirit, so it is necessary to awaken to the awareness of the Spirit. It is also necessary for us, as Spiritualists, to be in tune with those from the Spirit World, and set an example of how to live a good life.

We should look at life as a business: You all have something to sell in the market of life. We, who are spiritualists, have to sell our religion and you must realise that the competition is high.

Simply, your personal objective in life may be of no interest to others unless they can see in you an advantage for themselves. Consequently, no one is really interested in you, that is, as a human being, unless you have such qualities which in some manner are appealing to them.

Therefore, we must build up our qualifications, our personal inventory of saleable assets. I have always said that we are the church and others who look at us connect us to the church, so if we go around with long faces then that is reflected to others. On the other hand, if we can show a happy face, with shining eyes, then surely that is how we should sell ourselves. The commodities are few but essential, we must educate ourselves in the sale of our goods, we must train ourselves to be skilful, just as any employer would if he wants perfection in what he sells. If we fail to do this then we will have nothing to offer in the market, with empty hands wanting to make a sale but with nothing to offer.

Certainly, schooling and training may appear to be laborious but, again, the question will be asked: What have you to offer?

In the past, we have neglected to prepare for a future. We have now realised that our products must improve if we want to compete in the market. An alert merchant is always looking for a new and larger market; he wants to know what is drawing the prospective buyer. The Church of England now knows that healing is what people want and know that it may have to look at clairvoyance in order to survive.

Figuratively speaking, we have coasted along without a care, without looking for new avenues to explore, and we know that all merchandise becomes shop-soiled, styles change and so the merchant has to make his goods attractive in appearance. So we must look at our churches, as all other religions are doing and make them attractive and a place where people want to be.

Yes, we must study the market, we must know what is going on in order to compete. We are Spiritualists and we should know how spiritual essence can help and guide us in all our affairs. We should look at our future with confidence and growing assurance. That is the hallmark of all successful, happy people.

Our Spiritualist religion brings about a change in our mental and emotional lives so that we may live a more successful, spiritual life, free from fear.

If you join any organisation, whether it is a political or a non-political movement, or if you join any church, you are expected, since you have committed yourself, to give that organisation one undred percent of your effort, I hope that you who are not members will think about becoming one and help put our church and our religion in good stead for the future. Remember, the strength of the church is in its members.

We have a lot to offer in the market of life. What extent would you go to for your religion? It can only be revealed by you alone. The trouble is that most of us are so afraid of failure that we go out of our way to avoid it and so we fail to learn the valuable lessons it has to offer.

Reading a magazine, I came across these words: "If a job is worth doing - it's worth doing badly."

Of course, I knew this could not be correct; in fact, I thought it was bad advice, but when you realise that success is built on a foundation of failures, you needn't be afraid of failing.

We start so very young in life actively trying to avoid criticism and punishment handed out by our parents and teachers that it seems that most of us are conditioned in childhood to have some fear of failure, and that fear travels with us into adulthood and holds us back; therefore, we never realise our true potentials.

Remember, there is a first time for everything; if the mountaineer never made a start, he would never get to the top of the mountain. Just imagine how he feels when the mountain is conquered and he can look back on his successful achievement. No matter how many times he stumbled on his way, the harder the struggle, the sweeter the success.

I expect you will have gathered by now that my aim is to try to inspire you to conquer your fear of failing and have a go at all the education courses available to you.

Start your philosophy, dot down your thoughts and sayings.
It may be weeks or months before they come to fruition, but once you begin, it is surprising how it becomes relevant; each little part growing to make a whole. Everything we read feeds our mind and goes into the storehouse - the memory.

The time has come to start and gather material for your next first service.

THE SEVEN PRINCIPLES OF SPIRITUALISM

According to our teachings, God is Spirit and the living motivating force in Man. Man is also Spirit and this Spirit is the same essence as the Divine Spirit, so Man is said to be the Son of God and that Man is born coming forth from God, the Divine Spirit, to exist as an individual or separate entity, but he is not entirely independent because, in virtue of his nature, he is linked with God for all eternity, forever and ever, no matter how spiritually low we fall.

On entering Earth life, the spirit takes on a physical body; the physical body is necessary to enable the spirit to function as an individual on Earth and acquire consciousness and a sense of awareness of the physical world. Earth life is merely a short phase in the existence of the spirit but it is very necessary to provide it with Earth experience, which will enable it to acquire a distinct personality and build up its moral character and develop a spiritual nature.

Spiritualism teaches us that we reap what we sow; that as we think here on Earth and how we live this life on Earth will determine our place in the next world. Our mind, we ourselves, will be our own judge and jury, no one will save you, as other religions would have you believe. People believe that a saviour will forgive them because they have been brought up to believe that God requires a fixed form of belief beside certain rituals such as baptisms and confirmation and prefer you to be teetotal and non-smoking. This is what most religions believe is the gateway to heaven and it has been a great help and comfort to many. This Idea of salvation by faith has been a crutch to the faithful but that's all it is and no more, because it's not true.

If we are Spirit - and we are because we come from the same source and must return - then how can our Father God, who we are told loves us, banish us to a place called 'hell'.

145

Spiritualism today reveals that it is not what we believe that makes for happiness in the life to come but what we are and how we live. When Man realises the truth that he himself must save himself, when he faces facts and does not obtain comfort from his false imaginings, then we Spiritualists will move forward; natural religion will replace supernatural religion.

The first of our seven principles, THE FATHERHOOD OF GOD, tells us that the universe is governed by mind, commonly called 'God'; all we have sensed or will sense is mind expressing itsself in some form or another.

The second principle, THE BROTHERHOOD OF MAN, tells us the existence and identity of the individual continues after the change called 'death'.

The third principle, COMMUNION OF SPIRITS AND THE MINISTRY OF ANGELS, says that, under suitable conditions, communication takes place between us on Earth and those in the Spirit World.

The fourth principle, THE CONTINOUS EXISTENCE OF THE HUMAN SOUL, says each individual reaps what he sows and takes his happiness or unhappiness into his new surroundings.

The fifth principle, PERSONAL RESPONSIBILITY, tells us each individual is his own saviour and he cannot look to someone else to bear his sins and suffer for his mistakes.

The sixth principle, COMPENSATION AND RETRIBUTION HEREAFTER FOR ALL THE GOOD AND EVIL DEEDS DONE ON EARTH, makes us aware that our conduct must be guided by the golden rule, first proclaimed by Confucius, of doing to others as we wish to be done to ourselves.

The seventh principle, ETERNAL PROGRESS OPEN TO EVERY HUMAN SOUL, explains clearly that the path of progress is never closed and there is no end to the advancement of the spirit.

The principles dispel despair and give a feeling of hope and satisfaction and emphasise how right Confucius was to compress ethics into doing to others as we would be done by. They make each and everyone responsible for deeds done and what consequences follow our thoughts and actions. What counts is what we are... and not what we think we are.

146

No one need despair as progress is open to all, even the worst being, by efforts to outgrow past wrongs by mental development.

So what has Spiritualism done for you?

For me, Spiritualism gave me the answers to the deeper problems of life and with this knowledge my life has been happier and I have obtained the mental contentment which satisfies me.

Spiritualism explains and clarifies so many problems. Spiritualists know that this life is such a small span in our journey onward. As far as our destiny is concerned, if everyone does his/her best, no more can be expected. Religious beliefs are for this world and mean nothing in the world to come, so everyone should do his or her best to infuse kindness, sympathy, justice and tolerance. They all make for increased happiness.

Spiritualism cannot be dismissed as being unimportant; in fact other religions now know that we have got it right!

Modern Spiritualism is in the light and its rays radiate love for all. It can be understood by young and old and is full of interest to the learned. Spiritualism is equally accessible to rich and poor alike; it will help you in your life; it makes you more aware; it explains many things; it simplifies many queries and doubts of past teachings.

The study of Spiritualism is endless and its various branches are full of interest. Those who understand Spiritualism have a clearer outlook on life; it bridges the gap between this world and those who have passed over and allows us a continued affinity with the unseen helpers.

The teaching of The Seven Principles, if followed, would put to an end all wars and talk of wars, sickness in body and mind and all troubles on this Earth and find a cure for the present state of the world today.

There is no need to arrive in the Spirit World spiritually bankrupted, for our teachings prepare you to arrive with some qualifications.

The teachings of Spiritualism are God's laws and cannot be changed. Spiritualism embraces all religions and all nationalities; its treasures cannot be bought or stolen and they do not decay. It goes back to the beginning of time and will have no end. It does not demand that you believe, without question, that we are seekers of the truth and as this truth begins to dominate our lives so comes that inner tranquillity and strength that accompanies knowledge and enables you to give a true assessment of everything which is part of our daily life.

What Spiritualism has to offer is proof 'that love is undying', that death cannot act as a prisoner for a spiritual being once it has escaped from this Earth. Love is the almighty link between the two worlds.

S - SYMPATHY - SIMPLICITY - SYMPATHETIC NATURE.

P - PEOPLE - INVOLVEMENT OF - PATIENCE - PLEDGE - PITY.

I - INTEGRITY- SPIRITUAL INTELLIGENCE.

R- RESPONSIBILITY - RELIABILITY.

I - INSIGHT TO LIFE AFTER DEATH - INVOLVEMENT.

T - TOLERANCE - TENDERNESS - TRUTH.

U - UNDERSTANDING - UPLIFTMENT.

A - ADVANCEMENT - ANGELS.

L - LIGHT OF MPDERN SPRITUALISM - LOVED ONES - LIFE HERE AND HEREAFTER.

I - IMMORTALITY- INSPIRATION.

S - SPIRIT.

T - TEST - TEST THE SPIRIT. IT WILL RESPOND.

I think that the first verse of hymn 162 in the SNU Hymn Book by Alex McLeod would make a good 8th principle:

"What's good and pure in any creed
I take it and make it mine;
Whatever serves a human need
I hold to be divine."

I have used this verse many times in a service.

THOUGHTS

Today, I let my thoughts dwell on God's love, power and justice. I hold thoughts of goodwill and harmony toward all. Thought is a vital, living force that we are beginning to find that we may term a "science of thought."

We may find, through the instrumentality of thought-force, that there is a creative power, not merely in the figurative sense, but a creative power in reality. Science is life elevated into thought and consequently transformed into thinking, or it is a thought carried into reality that has passed and been transmitted into life and therein fully attested and certified by life itself; therefore, thinking becomes life.

My mind, to me, is a kingdom and so if my mind becomes a kingdom then I rule my kingdom; I am in control of my thoughts and have the power to keep the peace in the kingdom of my mind.

I know that the power of the Great Spirit is greater than any material power.

To dwell conscientiously upon God's presence ever with us is to draw strength and assurance from this realisation. To know that we are never alone, in any kind of need, is to know the strength which supports and maintains us and gives us new courage and confidence to go on. We know that the healing ministers from the Spirit World give strength to our limbs and power to our whole being and at the very least can bring us peace and a calming effect.

There is no substitute for spending time with the healing ministers who attune with their Earthly channels to bring relief to someone who is in need of help. What a great gift. What a sight that would be! What joy that would bring! We are reminded that God works in surprising ways to accomplish his purpose.

Today, on the news, a large amount of gold and silver coins had been discovered by treasure hunters, which causes us to dream about finding similar riches. I have written many times about the gifts of the Spirit and how priceless they are. We, as Spiritualists,

149

should be on a different treasure hunt. What we seek does not consist of silver or gold, rather our quest is to gather the precious gems of insight so that we might gain the insight and understanding of the Spirit at work through us.

Have you found a place in God's service where you can be used? You may have to be content with a small beginning but your attitude will determine your success, for it is never too late to become the person you want to be. Start today to initiate needed changes in your thinking and in your life, dwell on the thought of self-improvement; everything will respond to the positive thought. You can change any situation. This good news is for everyone who will receive it as a faculty of logical thinking.

The reason is, at the same time, a power of endless progressive development. When a thought enters the mind it becomes a piece of knowledge. It may be incomplete but it is now a thought waiting to be expressed. The journey of life is like any other journey, it is important to enjoy every step of the way, it is important that we enjoy everything and relish every moment as we journey into our future. We must prepare for any situation that might occur, so let every moment of your life be happy and in tune with the infinite love of God.

We are ever reminded that life is incredibly fragile; our purpose is not to live successful, happy lives but to realise the shortness of life so that we may grow in wisdom.

As an octogenarian, I know that I cannot live my material life again, but I am going to live a new way of life every day that I have yet to come. I cannot retrieve all the time that I have wasted but I will use the rest of the time that I have left to enjoy the privilege of controlling my free time during my days and evenings.

Getting old is not for the faint hearted; while we are getting older physically, we do not have to get old in our outlook. We live in a disposable culture that dismisses senior citizens as set in their ways and out of touch. Elderly people prove otherwise by demonstrating that while age isn't convenient or comfortable, it can be productive by focusing on the 'can do' instead of the 'use to do'. It gives the next generation a blueprint to follow.

Your life today is more than what happened yesterday, it is about what you do with what happened yesterday. There is much that God has placed on your way for you to enjoy as you go through life. A meaningful life is one that has significance in the lives of others you help to meet their needs and solve their problems. This should be your guiding principle in life, and in this very inspiring and captivating thought, we have the ability to transform our lives and make them go in a particular direction, remembering that what we do in this life echoes into eternity.

Now, in concluding our development of the human mind, to which our investigations have, step by step, been leading us, we need to be in a position to see beyond the horizon. If the conflicts of the present life are to be met with patience and endurance, although another line of thought may perhaps lead us more directly to the end we have in view.

We have to determine the survival of the personality in the same way that we determine whether another person in the body is conscious. We are trying to prove that Spirit exists.

Socrates said: "All men's souls are immortal, but the souls of the righteous are immortal and divine" and "Cicero" said: "The life of the dead is placed in the memory of the living."

This is the secret of a worry-free life. God desires all men to lead a quiet, peaceable life. You are responsible to God and the country where you live to seek its peace. What you have to do, as individuals, is to intercede for the progress and prosperity and preservation of the country where you live. True peace is the harmonious expression of love and comes from within. Before peace can come to the world, love must be found in every individual's life, our lives should be ones of giving and receiving. We are aware that some take and never give. A meaningful life is one that has significance in the lives of others. Remember, you are part of a story that shapes this world. Each day can be special and of great value; it can be another step in our growth and spiritual unfoldment. Always we can carry with us thoughts and attitudes that are positive and enlightening.

We must consider the evidence for the existence of Spirit from the stories of those who visit us here.

151

The Dalai Lama said: "Remembering that sometimes not getting what you want is a wonderful stroke of luck."

Today Is My Day

Today my thoughts are centred on expecting only the best
and giving only the best.

Today my mind and heart are open to new opportunities,
and I make the most out of every situation.

Today I will smile and act enthusiastically in everything I do.
I will make every person I meet feel important, and
I will show them I care.

Today my confidence is high and I am willing to step out
and take a chance.
I speak freely to all those I meet.
I know I have something valuable to contribute,
I expect results today and my time is well invested.

Today I am one step closer to achieving my goal and dreams.
I always keep my eyes focused on success
and prosperity.
Today I will sow good seeds so that I will reap my harvest of Reward.

Today is my day!!!

Author unknown

TIME FLIES

They say that time flies when your having fun. As an octogenarian, I can tell you that time goes at different speeds. When I was younger and working, time seemed to drag; in fact, my boss used to say he was employing clock watchers, but then I think: "How did I arrive at this age - eighty-four?" I cannot believe how old I have got; age seems to have crept up on me overnight.

Let me tell you, there is nothing grand in getting old, but it's nice to be able to look back at the good things that have happened in my life. I have had a good marriage, although it took two to achieve it, but they say "If at first you don't succeed, try, try again." In my case, it has been wonderful; I have three sons, all different but I love them to bits. I have been lucky in my employment - I served as an apprentice clicker in a shoe factory, then at an engineering company then as a hospital porter and a kitchen hand. I became a minister and a prison chaplain until the age of eighty-one and now a little older, I have written two books, so I expect it could be said that I am an author. My next book will be attributed to my grandson, reliving the stories told to him at bedtime.

Although we cannot get around as we used to do, we are blessed in friendship with Karen and David. I still look back full of the joys to go on living, and you could say its bonus time, and I realise that I live with the knowledge that my wife Joyce and I will carry on until God calls us to a higher ministry.

You might ask why God has put us in a world where time is a problem and everything ages and decays all around us. What is new and very up-to-date is discarded as obsolete almost immediately, so now we realise that only the things of the Spirit are eternal and last forever. Life on Earth is a progression through experiences which have the potential to lead us back to our creator, to be conscious that the God-spirit is all around us, leading us through the tough times in our lives.

I still recall the wasted years of the past and yet I know that, in an instance, God can turn this loss to gain and I endeavour to keep in constant attunment with my spirit helpers, seeking advice and help as long as I need it.

I sit here looking out into the garden, which I have named "My Memory Garden" because some of the plants were given to me by friends and relations, some who are now in the Spirit World and I know that I shall not forget them, for when I take a walk around and look at them, I remember they came with love from those who gave them to me. I thank God for all that he has given me, and this is best described by Ralph Waldo Emerson:

> *For each new morning with its light,*
> *For rest and shelter of the night,*
> *For health and food, for love and friends,*
> *For everything*
> *Thy goodness sends.*

WALK WITH GOD

There is a song with words that go: "I'll walk with God from this day on" and if there is such a thing, it would mean that one is in direct contact with the Great Spirit. I believe that the Divine Spirit works with individuals who want to be under direct inspiration. The spirit of God works through instruments and agencies of human societies.

There is a special joy for those who experience working with the Spirit and though they not know how, it is of great joy to be able to communicate with Spirit, who is dealing with human souls.

One thing is important if we are to receive the words that Spirit offers to us: We need space within so that this enlightening encounter with the Spirit can take place.

We are called as channels of listening and receiving the messages from our loved ones and friends in the World of Spirit and we must find time in our schedule to just stop what we are doing so that we can attune ourselves to the Spirit as it brings a peace and a calming effect. Being still, enjoying receiving and being refreshed and renewed by the Spirit is to a great extent a matter of practice.

The light of understanding is being revealed in many places. Our spirit friends are ever near to us, to guide and sustain our steps through this life, but many of us have taken the wrong pathway in life and struggle to handle our problems on our own. Never forget that our spirit friends are ever near to guide and help us to get back in step so that we can stride out with confidence having experienced the richness of spiritual wisdom.

Remember, every charitable act is a stepping stone towards your spiritual future.

As we travel through our everyday lives, we are guided by those from the Spirit Realm. We may use other terms, like "an

155

unseen force", or "guiding hand" but love is the almighty link, so our loved ones, who are ever close, guide and inspire us from the World of Spirit, helping us to charter a course on our pathway of life, which may seem to be fraught with many dangers, seen and unseen. But we have been given the power of positive thought which can, if we want it to, make us think that every day, things will be better in every way.

It is important that our thoughts, words and deeds are pure as they can have devastating effects on oneself and on others. Our thoughts can be used for good or ill, but every thought sent out will return in like manner, as thoughts are living things.

Genuine investigations will lead to amazing discoveries. I am grateful for the divinely given ability to choose what course I will take in life. I give thanks to the guidance from Spirit and keep attuned as I choose to follow spirit ways. Each day can be special and of great value. Life, for me, is delightful and full of interest, whether I am alone or in company, because I go about my day with a singing heart and a receptive spirit that looks for the good. I keep attuned and become aware of new avenues of good, new and more productive ways of thinking and acting as they are revealed to me.

As we walk with God, we receive the gift of everlasting love and warmth of assurance. We find comfort and peace, we regain our sense of security and realise that we can never be separated in Spirit from those we love. The strength of God is our strength and helps us to meet life today, ready for the next step that has been prepared for us.

Personally, I regard the fact of survival after death as being scientifically proved; the evidence is so plentiful. We see ourselves and our dear ones as travellers on the path of life. We see that those who pass from life really pass into life and any sense of loss is alleviated, grief disappears and we feel the presence of deep peace, comfort and the love of God. We see that all of life's experiences are important to the whole and what's more, God's compassionate love always leads us in the way of abundant blessings and perfect fulfilment of our needs.

Always remember that you, the real you, is a spirit and not a body and while we are in this world, each and every one of us is a soul, a spiritual being inside this physical costume of the human body.

When we lose a loved one, we mourn but we do not sorrow, as if there is no hope, we may never know why this misfortune happened to us, but we do know that whatever comes our way has the blessings of the Great Spirit.

Life is a mission to discover, comprehend and intellectually master that small part of the divine law. There is a need for us to find an aim in life, which tends to express itself in all round practical efficiency. So, if I should feel uncertain about my life, I give thanks to the never failing help from the Spirit and receive my right direction. Every day is part of our journey of life and we are encouraged and sustained, regardless of delays and upsets.

Each day can be special and of greater value, it can be another step in our growth and spiritual enfoldment. I rejoice in the infinite possibilities of life. Can there be any real prospects without the fundamental message which we are all eagerly waiting for, the secret that will bring inner peace and that there is no death? That secret may be most effectively communicated through the testimony of those who have experienced it.

To know that we walk with God and that our pathway is always peaceful and protected can change the way we may have viewed our lives and our daily actions. This life that has been given us is immortal. We live right here and now, moment by moment, breath by breath, by virtue of divine life and I am filled with new courage and new strength.

This courage makes me a strong person, a person whose outlook is positive and hopeful; I can meet all things knowing that I can depend on my helpers from the World of Spirit and in that trusting confidence, with its dreams of infinite love, I realise that as I change my thinking, I change my life. We have now reached the culminating point that the supreme life which, according to what has already been said, is the primary source of all other life.

This poem is by Hannah More (1785):

In spite of what the Scripture teaches,
In spite of all the parson preaches,
This world (indeed I've thought so long)
Is rul'd methinks, extremely wrong.

This world, which clouds thy soul with doubts,
Is but a carpet inside out.

So when on earth things look but odd,
They're working still some scheme of God.

POEM
BY JOYCE PICKERSGILL

I'm top of the tree,
My dad said to me
When I was small,
What does that mean, thought I,
We're not rich at all.

I remember the laughter and the fun,
When the day's work was done.
He would tell us a tale, of days gone by,
With a twinkle in his eye.

When the punchline came,
We knew we'd been had,
Such was the humour of our dad.

The love that shone from his rosy face,
I thought lost forever,
Until that day of grace.

When he returned from above,
To share my joy, with a new found love.
Someone who could describe to me,
The wonders of a life to be.

POEMS
BY MINISTER SIDNEY PICKERSGILL

MY WIFE

There is no task too hard for her to undertake,
She never grumbles if I fail to wake.
Her temper nor her voice breaks the silent air,
She never thinks of herself, others take first place.
She is never demanding, but she is a little coy,
God knows, I'll always love her, she is my pride and Joyce.

A PRAYER

Pray for help, God understands,
and will do his best for you.
But remember this, someone else,
May pray for the opposite to you.

Our Father has now to decide,
Who needs the blessing most.
So if it's you he cannot help,
He'll suffer at your side.

The path of life may be hard and long,
Sometimes you may be near despair.
Close your eyes, ask him again,
You may feel his presence near.

GOD'S HOUSE
The house of God is open,
Come in, there's room for you.

Join with others who seek, to rest,
For one small moment, close to his Breast

Give unto him your life your all?
He's the one that lifts you, when you fall.

Do his will from day to day,
Try to follow, in his way.

He will not fail you, he will be your guide,
until you're safely by his side.

HEALING
Let the healing water flow, nourished and fed by thee.
Faith supports us, by faith we stand, instruments of the healing
hands.

Come the ones who are sick, the healer's hands may do the trick,
Our Heavenly Father sends his love, with the angels from their
bright homes above.

These poems were composed the late Herbert Fletcher, past President of Dewsbury Church, who left them to me in his will.

SIGNS AND SYMBOLS

Often those who dwell on high,
Can feel our pain or hear our sigh.
Sense our loneliness and grief,
And seek to bring us some relief.

In many ways they seek to aid,
With messages that are relayed.
By guides and mediums, speakers too,
Who thus bring comfort down to you.

Signs and symbols sent from above,
Are often tokens of great love.
Mental impressions from memory's pages,
That still live on throughout life's stages.

For though we cannot see or hear,
The spirit forms of those held dear.
And to their presence we are blind,
We can, through the great power of the mind,
Receive their thoughts and loving greetings,
When we get together at our meetings.

****

Truth is truth where're 'tis found,
Though this be not on hallowed ground.
You can hitch your wagon to a star,
but without God's help, you'll not get far.

SEEDS

God makes flowers in many hues,
Various yellows, reds and blues.
Some there are grow big and tall,
Others we know are very small.
But each one grows to God's great plan,
Finding a corner where it can.
The seeds, they oft' float around,
Hoping to find some fertile ground.
The ways in which these seeds are sown,
Vary so much - great wisdom is shown.
The use of wind, even insects' wings,
To gain their ends, they use many things.
For often the scraping of bird beaks,
Deposits the seed in a spot it seeks.
Maybe the mistletoe on oaken bough,
Was part of a meal that escaped somehow?
And when a bird, a moment spent,
The opportunity was heaven sent.
The various weeds we so often curse,
Are each dedicated to disperse.
Their seeds all seek propagation,
And cover the world with vegetation.
May each species find beauty in birth,
To add to the glory of Mother Earth.

SPIRIT VOICES

Down through all the vibrant spaces,
Cometh spirit thoughts tonight.
Using guides of many races,
Helping us to see the light.
Telling us of life hereafter,
And of those who've left our Earth.
Of their joy and happy laughter,
Children of a second birth.

Oft' they bring a loving greeting,
Bidding us to watch and pray.
Very soon we'll all be meeting,
When we've shed our Earthly clay.
Theirs the voice of living spirit,
Quickening souls who never die.
Paying us a fleeting visit,
From their spirit homes on high.

Coming like the dawning daylight,
Lighting up our Earthly day.
Teaching that, to all who do right,
The Great Spirit will repay.
For when mortal days are ended,
And our Earthly strivings cease.
With all friends so truly blended,
We shall find eternal peace.

THE CHURCH OF SPIRIT

In our Church of Spirit, there is room for you,
We extend a welcome that is warm and true.
Why should you be lonely, why for friendship sigh
When our Church of Spirit can your wants supply?

'Mid the thoughts of Spirit, will be some for you,
Warm as summer sunshine, sweet as morning dew.
Why should you be fearful, why be overwrought?
Help can come from Spirit, by the power of thought.

In the work of Spirit, there's a task for you,
Such as even angels might rejoice to do.
Why stand idly dreaming of some life work grand,
When the field of Spirit needs your helping hand?

Seek and find the talent that you may command,
Tread the path of service, join our healing band.
Share the love of Spirit with your fellow man,
Help uplift the fallen, do what good you can.

In the world of Spirit, there's a place for you,
Glorious, bright and joyous, calm and peaceful too.
When life's tasks are over and your journey ends,
You will meet your loved ones and your erstwhile friends.

Chorus
Share our blessings, each and every one,
Share our blessings, see what God has done.
Share our blessings, count them one by one,
And it will surprise you what the Lord has done.

(Can be sung to the tune of 'Count Your Blessings')

THANKFULNESS

Though our service soon is ending,
And from church we now must go.
Still our thoughts are ever blending,
With the friends we used to know.

Ever blending, ever blending,
With the friends we used to know,
Thank all for the peace and healing,
We have found within these doors,
And the kindly, loving feeling ,
Helps to make the spirit soar.

Loving feeling, loving feeling,
Helps to make the spirit soar.
So we sing our final greeting,
Ere we wend our homeward way,

Earthly time is all too fleeting,
Thankyou for a lovely day,
All too fleeting, all too fleeting,
Thankyou for a lovely day

THOUGHTS

If thoughts are living things that fly,
They'll circle the Earth and reach the sky.
They'll live and move and have their being,
So let us take care in seeing.
The ones we send out on their way,
Will help to brighten up each day.

A QUOTE:

There's lots that's wrong in our worldly life,
We pray to God, amend it.
Man is the cause of all our strife,
So he is the one who can end it.

A PRINCIPLE BY HERBERT FLETCHER:

Laws must exist, so God decreed,
That man must pay for each misdeed.
Evil acts bring retribution,
But goodly deeds their compensation.

For within each one we know,
The voice of conscience tells us so.
Whether we've good or bad intent.
When we're on some action bent.

So let us all, our conscience hear,
And keep its contents crystal cear.
Mental ease will help our health,
Thus adding to our store of wealth.